PANORAMA
OF
HARAPPAN CIVILIZATION

PANORAMA
OF
HARAPPAN CIVILIZATION

D.P. Sharma

Madhuri Sharma

Kaveri Books

New Delhi-110002

ISBN: 978-81-7479-057-6
Edition 2019

Photo Courtesy:
National Museum, New Delhi and
Archaeological Survey of India, New Delhi

Published by
Kaveri Books
4832/24, Ansari Road
New Delhi-110002 (India)
Tel: 011-47072321
E-mail: kaveribooks@gmail.com
Website: www.kaveribooks.com

Laser Typesetting by :
Delta Book World, Delhi

PRINTED IN INDIA

Dedicated to Guru
Late Prof G.R. Sharma

Acknowledgements

My sincere thanks to Dr. B.L. Nagarch, Ex-Director Exploration and Excavation of A.S.I. now expert of physical verification of National Museum of India and also to Dr. Neeru Misra, Director I.C.C.R. presently working as Director under U.N.D.P. Delhi for editing the manuscript and making several valuable suggestions. Dr. Ravindra Deo Choudhury, D.G. National Museum, New Delhi and Dr. Nayanjot Lahiri, Alok Tripathi, Prof Vibha Tripathi, Miss Maushumi Chatterji, Prof O.P. Yadav, Dr. R.R. Singh Chauhan, Shobika, Deepti Grover, Snigdha Sinha, Pooja, Supriya, Sanjib Kumar Singh, Miss Rohini Pande, Dr. Manoj, S. N. Pathak, Ashish Kumar and K.C. Nauriyal for various types of academic help. I am equally grateful to B.B. Lal, J.P. Joshi both ex-D.G.A.S.I., Dr. S.R. Rao, R.S. Bisht, Amrendra Nath, Madhubala and Dharamveer Sharma, all excavators of Kalibangan, Surkotada, Lothal, Dholavira, Rakhigarhi, Dhalewan and Mandi respectively for use of the photos of the objects in their collections. J.C. Arora, Photo Officer and Tajveer Singh of the National Museum did the photography of this publication. The drawings and sketches of this publication were prepared by my daughters Kadambini (Architect) and Devangana. Raju Gharai, Raj Bisht, Sangam Jatti and Bhavana did the typing work of this manuscript. The photographs used here are by courtesy of G.L. Possehl, S.P. Gupta, H. Kondo, J.P. Joshi, Mark Kenoyer , B.B. Lal, R.S. Bisht, Amrendra Nath, K.N. Dikshit, V. Shinde and Madhubala Sharma. We wrote this book in simple language for the students of Art History, Ancient Indian History, Archaeology and also for them who are appearing in Indian Civil Services examinations.

Deo Prakash Sharma
Head of Harappan Collection,
National Museum, Janpath,
New Delhi - 110011.

Preface

During 1983-84, while studying at the Institute of Archaeology, London, Prof. Ian Glover taught me Harappan Archaeology. After obtaining the M.A. degree in Archaeology from London University I joined the National Museum on 5th January 1985 as Dy. Keeper (Prehistory and Archaeology). I took charge of Harappan Antiquities in the National Museum from late Shri L.A. Narain who was then the Dy. Director of the National Museum. I have been incharge of the Harappan Antiquities for the last seventeen years. During my stay in the National Museum I came in contact with Harappan Archaeologists from all over the world and learnt a lot about the Harappan archaeology. By the blessings of and contacts with Dr. S.P. Gupta and late Dr. Shashi Asthana-both former Assistant Directors of National Museum- I came to know more about the Harappan Archaeology. During 1994-1995 I was nominated as the main curator of the exhibition on "India and Indus Civilization," which was part of an event in the third world Archaeological congress held in Delhi. During this exhibition I came in contact with Harappan Archaeologists like B.B. Lal, R.C. Tripathi, B.K. Thapar, J.P. Joshi, K.N. Dikshit, M.K. Dhavlikar, R.S. Bisht, Vasant Shinde, S.V. Sonawane, V.N. Misra, S.R. Rao, Alok Tripathi,

M. Lal, Madhubala, Shereen Ratnagar, Jaya Menon, D.V. Sharma, A.K. Sinha, Ravi Korisettar, B.K. Saran, A.K. Sharma, J.N. Pal, D.K. Chakrabarti and J.N. Pande. I took over the charge of the Harappan Antiquities of the Indian sites from R.S. Bisht.

During 2000-2001, the Archaeological Survey of India and National Museum jointly set up a new permanent Harappan Gallery at the National Museum and I was the main coordinator and Mrs. Komal Anand, Ex-D.G.A.S.I. was the chairperson. During this period I again came in contact with Harappan Archaeologists like B.B. Lal, S.P. Gupta, S.R.Rao, R.S. Bisht, Amrendra Nath, M.N. Deshpande, Madhubala, K.N. Dikshit, Bhuvan Vikram, Late Ajay Shankar, M.C. Joshi, Nayanjot Lahiri and J.P. Joshi, and learnt many new things from them.

During 2001, I was involved in the Indus Valley exhibition, held in Japan. Mr. R.S. Bisht and H. Kondo were incharge of this exhibition. I visited Tokyo (Japan) and organized the Indus exhibition at Nagoya. During my stay there I also examined the Harappan antiquities collections of Pakistan, India and British Museum.

During 1990, I wrote my first book "Indus Valley Activity book", which is currently being revised by me. During 1999, I wrote my second book "Bharat and Sindh Sabhyata" in Hindi.

According to S.P. Gupta and B.B. Lal, Harappan Civilization was the gift of two rivers– the Indus and Saraswati. Gupta has recently reported around 1048 Harappan sites, which are located on the dried-up course of Saraswati. According to Possehl (2000), J.P. Joshi (2001), S.P. Gupta (2001) and the present author, the following are the statistics of Harappan sites in North Western part of South Asia.

Total No. of Harappan and its associated sites		2658
Harappan sites on Saraswati	=	1048
Harappan associated sites in the region of north-western South Asia other than Saraswati region	=	1610

This book deals with a few rare Harappan art objects and the new discoveries of Harappan sites. The first chapter is on Early Harappan (c 3500-2700 B.C.) Cultures. So far 483 early Harappan sites have been reported from the north-western regions of south Asia. Of these seventy four early Harappan sites have been excavated. The early Harappan stage precedes the urbanization of Mature Harappan. The various regional phases in the early Harappan are as follows: (1) Amri-Nal (2) Kulli Mehi (3) Kot diji (4) Damb Sadaat (5) Sothi-Siswal.

Togau phase (c 4300-3800 B.C.) Kechi Beg phase (c. 3800-3200 B.C.), Hakra Ware phase (c 3800-3200 B.C.) and Ravi Ware phase (c 3600-3300 B.C.) are preludes to the early Harappan Chalcolithic sites.

The second chapter is on Harappan civilization (c 2700-2000 B.C.). During the last eighty-two years more than 2658 Harappans and their associated sites have been reported in south Asia and around 203 Harappan sites have been excavated. In 1917 A.D. the Italian scholar Lugi Pio Tessitori had excavated Kalibangan and later on around 1920-21 Harappa and Mohenjo-daro were excavated. The total area of Harappan civilization is 1.6 million sq.k.m. Ganweriwala situated on the bank of river Saraswati (Hakra) is the largest Mature Harappan site and it covers an area of 250 hectares. The National Museum, New Delhi, has a collection of 4800 Harappan artifacts. The rock-cut reservoir recently discovered at Dholavira suggests a unique water management. According to B.B. Lal, J.P. Joshi, R.S. Bisht,

S.P. Gupta, Shereen Ratnagar and Nayanjot Lahiri the Aryan invasion theory of massacre at Harappan sites does not hold any ground.

The third chapter is on the stone sculptures discovered from Dholavira, Mohenjo-daro and Harappa. A seated fragmentary head-less priest from Dholavira is the largest (37cm.) among all the stone images of Harappan sites. Some rare stone images are a priest's bust and head from Mohenjo-daro and a male torso and a dancer from Harappa.

The fourth chapter is on the Bronze images from the Harappan sites. A few rare bronze images are those of a dancing girl, a buffalo from Mohenjo-daro and three animals from Diamabad. A small bronze chariot from Mohenjo-daro and a huge chariot from Diamabad are also interesting.

The fifth chapter is on the Terracotta figurines that include male and female, animal and bird figurines from Harappan sites.

The sixth chapter is on seals, sealings and copper tablets. So far 5515 inscribed objects have been reported from Harappan sites.

The seventh chapter is on Mature Harappan Jewellery.

At the end of this book there is a list of Radio Carbon dates and a select bibliography of Harappan Archaeology.

Deo Prakash Sharma
National Museum, New Delhi.

Contents

1

Early Harappan

Neolithic sites like Mehrgarh and Cambay in the Indus region are a prelude the early Harappan in the Indus-Saraswati regions. During early Harappan period settlement pattern average size increase and growth and expansion of early Harappan to the east in Rajasthan, Jammu, Gujarat, Punjab, Haryana and western Uttar Pradesh. [Fig.1 (a,b)]. So far 483 early Harappan sites have been reported in India and Pakistan. An average site size of early Harappan is 5.49 hectares. Seventy-four early Harappan sites have had some excavation. The ceramics following the Kechi Beg / Hakra ware phase will be called the early Harappan (Pre Harappan). The Early Harappan stage precedes the urbanization of mature Harappan civilization in the greater Indus- Saraswati region with a short (100 or 50 years) transitional stage in some places separating them. Nausharo, Dhalewan, Rakhigarhi early phase and Kunal represent the transitional stage (circa 2800- 2700 B.C.) between the early and mature Harappan. [Fig.2 (a,b)].

The early Harappan period (circa 3500- 2700 B. C.) made up of four regional phases that are generally thought to be contemporary with one other are the Amri-Nal phase,

Fig. 1a : First farming stone to C.6000-4500 B.C., Mehrgarh, Pakistan collection photograph after Kondo, 2001

Fig. 1b : Neolithic period stone objects PdIA C.7000-6000 B.C. Mehrgarh, Pakistan Archaeology Department photograph after Kondo, 2001

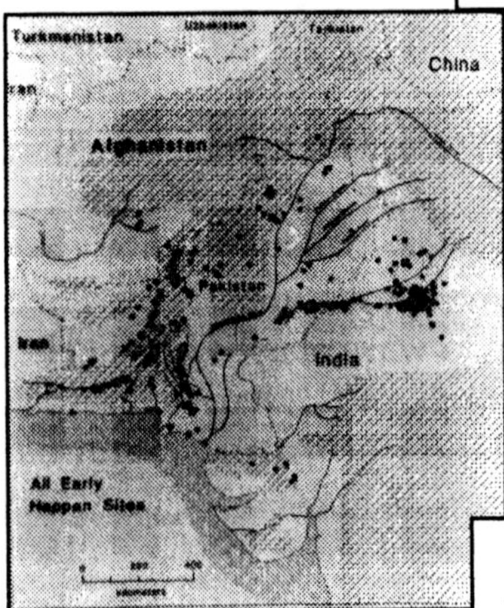

Fig. 2a : Map showing Early Harappan village chalcolithic sites in north west part of South Asia C-3500-2800 B.C. N.N 2/6 2000 A.D. Photograph after Possehl, 2000.

Fig. 2b : Silver Jewellery, 2800-2700 B.C. Kunal, National Museum, New Delhi collection loan from Haryana State Archaeology Department, Chandigarh

the Kot Dijian phase, the Damb Sadaat phase and the Sothi-Siswal phase. The transitional stage between the Early and Mature Harappan was a period of rapid changes and during this period [circa 2700 - 2600 B.C.] the urban features of the Harappan civilization came into being.

This short transitional period of rapid *paroxysmal* changes occupied the century from [circa 2700- 2600 B.C.] and during this period culture changes took place.

The Absolute Chronology of Harappan Age

Stage One: Beginnings of Village farming Communities and Pastoral Camps

Kili Ghul Mohammad Phase	C.8000-5000 BC
Burj Basket-marked Phase	C.5000-4300 BC

Stage Two: Developed Village farming Communities and Pastoral Societies

Togau Phase	C.4300-3800 BC
**Kechi Beg Phase	C.3800-3200 BC
**Hakra Wares Phase	C.3800-3200 BC
Ravi Phase	C.3600-3300 BC

Stage Three: Early Harappan four Phases thought to have been generally contemporaneous

Amri-Nal Phase	C.3500-2700 BC
Kot Dijian Phase	C.3100-2700 BC
Sothi-Siswal Phase	C.3100-2700 BC
Damb Sadaat Phase	C.3100-2700 BC

**The Kechi Beg and Hakra Wares Phases are thought to have been generally contemporaneous.

Stage Four

(a) Early-Mature Harappan Transition C.2700-2600 BC

(b) Copper hoard and O.C.P tradition C.2800-1500 BC

Stage Five: Mature Harappan five Phases thought to have been generally contemporaneous

Sindhi Harappan Phase	C.2700-2000 BC
Kulli Harappan Phase	C.2700-2000 BC
Sorath Harappan Phase	C.2600-2000 BC
Punjabi Harappan Phase	C.2700-2000 BC
Eastern Harappan Phase	C.2600-2000 BC

Two related Phases in adjacent regions thought to be generally contemporaneous with the mature Harappan

Quetta Phase	C.2560-2000 BC
Late Kot Diji Phase	C.2600-2000 BC

Stage Six: Post-urban Harappan

Jhukar Phase	C.2000-1800 BC
Early Pirak Phase	C.2000-1000 BC
Late Sorath Harappan Phase	C.2000-1600 BC
Lustrous Red Ware Phase	C.2000-1400 BC
Cemetery H Phase	C.2000-1500 BC
Swat Valley Period IV	C.1650-1300 BC
Late Harappan Phase in Haryana and Western Uttar Pradesh	C.2000-1500 BC
Late Harappan-Painted Grey Ware Overlap Phase	C.1600-1500 BC
Early Gandhara Grave Culture Phase	C.1900-1000 BC

Stage Seven: Early Iron Age of Northern India and Pakistan

Late Pirak, Allahdino, Lahura-Deo	C.2000-1700 BC

Painted Grey Ware	C.1600-500 BC
Late Gandharan Grave Culture	C.1000-600 BC

AMRI-NAL EARLY HARAPPAN PHASE

Early Harappan Amri-Nal phase proposed chronology is circa c 3500- 2700 B.C. So far 143 Amri-Nal sites have been discovered in the north-west part of south Asia. The important excavated Amri-Nal phase sites are Amri, Anjira, Balakot, Dholavira early phase , Nagwada I, Nal, Nundara, Togau, Banawali, Ghazshah and Surkotada.

Nal polychrome ceramics are the best and most attractive wares of the early Harappan period [Fig.3 (a,b)]. These are fine wares but tend to have been fired buff to pink. The slips have a tendency to be very light, buff or

Fig. 3a : Polychrome Ceramic, C. 3200-2800 B.C., Nal, National Museum, New Delhi Collection

Fig. 3b : Polychrome Ceramic, C. 2800-2700 B.C. Banawali, National Museum, New Delhi Collection

weak red, giving a tint to the surface rather than a dense over-all colour. The main vessels are a canister and a straight sides bowl with a simple, knife-edged rim. These were painted in black geometric designs or with realistically rendered animals antelopes, goats, fish, scorpion, birds and canids. The polychrome infilling of these designs include the use of white over a black slip which is also known in other potteries of early Harappan period. White painting is mostly a hall-mark in the entire early Harappan period ceramics. (Fig.4)

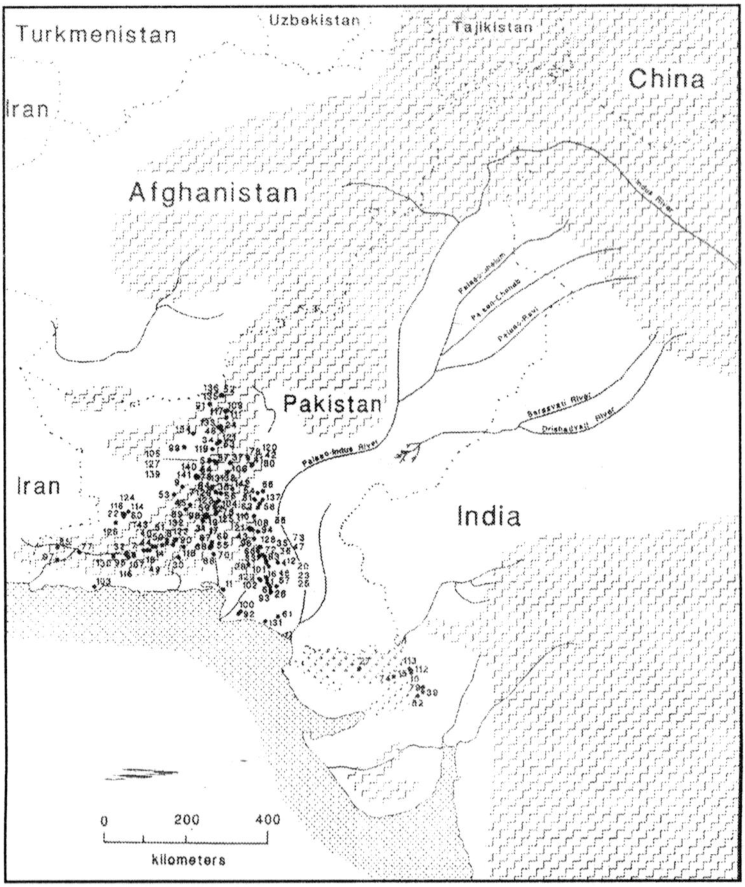

Fig. 4 : Map of sites of the Amri-Nal Phase after Possehl : 2000

The Amri ceramics is made of extremely well-made fine wares mostly fired light red or buff. Red and buff slips with black painting are also found. The designs are geometric and curvilinear. The main shapes of Amri ceramics are open bowls and jars and tall vases with special characteristics of Nal designs concentric circle and sigma. Besides these, there are symbols, bird and V shaped signs. A few pots of Nal have the symbol of Unicorn.

Amri-Nal phase pottery was also reported from Padri Surkotada, Nagwada, Bhamaria, Santhli, Motipipli and Harthar-no Timbo-all in Gujarat. The early Harappan ceramics of period I at Dholavira include the wheel-made red to pink wares, comb incised wares and deep-fished sniff jars. Slips of these ceramics are in red and darker tones. The painting is in dark and white which is a typical characteristic of the early Harappans. Nagwada is another Amri-Nal type site in Gujarat. The potteries from Nagwada burial is of the Amri type. The main shapes are tall vases dish on stand type and featureless rims; some ceramics are red slipped pot with white painting like the Sothi Siswal type (Fig.5).

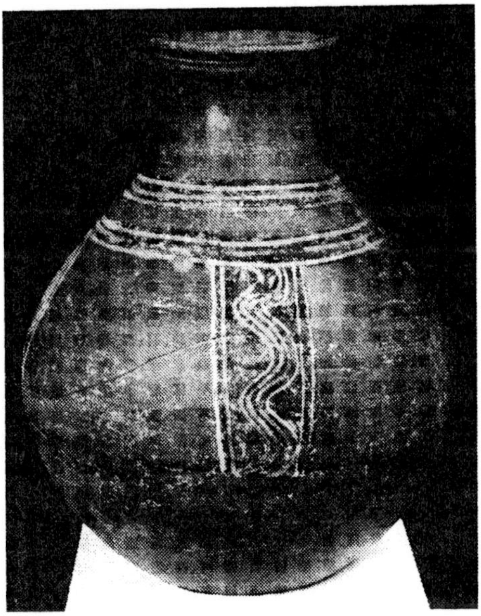

Fig. 5 : Bichrome Ceramics C. 2800-2700 B.C. (Early Harappan period) Nagwada, Gujrat, M.S. University Baroda, Neg No. 2118-95

The Kot Diji phase of Northern Sindh

Kot Diji is another early Harappan site in Pakistan. The Kot Diji ceramics are distinct from Amri- Nal ceramics. There are some common shapes and decorative designs. So far around 114 Kot Diji sites have been reported and the average site size is 6.31 hectares. The Kot Diji ceramic is of thin light weight with some paring of vessels walls to thin them while pots were still wet and leathery. The ring base is not fine. The pottery is decorated with horned deity (*Proto-siva*). The pottery has fine smoothened surfaces. The main types of Kot Diji ceramic complex are Bhoot ware, Wet ware, Micacious-sand Rusticated ware and Quetta ware (Fig. 6).

Fig. 6 : Horned deity depiction on Pot, Circa 2800-2700 B.C., Kotdiji, National Museum, Karachi Collection

Bhoot ware has a deeply grooved finish surface first identified at site Bhoot in Cholistan. The main shape are small globular pots. These pots are never burnished and are quite porous. The globular pots of Bhoot ware are water containers, the grooves functionally increasing the surface area of the vessel enhancing the cooling effect achieved by the evaporation of water from the vessel surface.

Wet ware has dendric pattern. Its surface was achieved by applying a thick slurry of viscose clay to the body of unfired or unfinished pots. These pots were then covered with wet cloths, which was lighted in a way that left the characteristic impression. Wet ware pattern pots are round and seem to be water containers.

Sand Rusticated wares have a thick slip of sandy clay applied to the body portion of the vessel. This type of pottery is also found in Sothi - Siswal and fabric B of Kalibangan.

The Damb Sadaat Phase of Baluchistan

There are thirty-eight Damb Sadaat sites and the average size is 2.64 hectares. The largest site is the Quetta Miri (23 hectares). The next largest site is Mundigak in Afghanistan. The important excavated sites of a Damb Sadaat phase are Quetta Miri, Mundigak and Damb Sadaat. The ceramics of Damb Sadaat phase are Quetta ware and Faiz Mahammod Grey ware. The Painted pottery is Quetta ceramics ware. The Faiz Mahammod Grey ware is fine. These ceramics were first baked as red buff ware in an oxidizing atmosphere and then refired under reducing condition to obtain the finished grey colour. It has black painting over grey. The Faiz Mahammod grey ware shares the common feature with Emiv grey ware of Shahi-tump of Iran (Fig.7).

Fig. 7 : Double Bull Pot Damb Sadaat Early Harappan Period

In the Quetta ware the most common motif is the stepped square. This was also noticed on Nal pottery. The painting on Quetta ware shows similarity with those of central Asia which are polychrome but Quetta is bichrome. The compartmented stamp-seals from Damb Sadaat phase of Baluchistan and central Asia are also alike. The stepped cross motif found on the Quetta ceramics has central Asian origin and identical ceramics was reported from Altyn depe in central Asia. The Damb Sadaat phase shows long distances trades with Baluchistan and central Asia.

SOTHI SISWAL PHASE OF EASTERN REGION

So far 158 Sothi- Siswal sites of the early Harappan period have been discovered in which 18 are excavated sites. Sothi, Nohar, Siswal, Kalibangan, Banawali, Rakhigarhi, Tarkhanewala Dera and Dhalewan are important Sothi-Siswal sites. B.K Thapar identified six fabrics of Sothi-Siswal which are designated A to F of Kalibangan. Kalibangan is a typical early Harappan Sothi-Siswal phase site (Fig. 8).

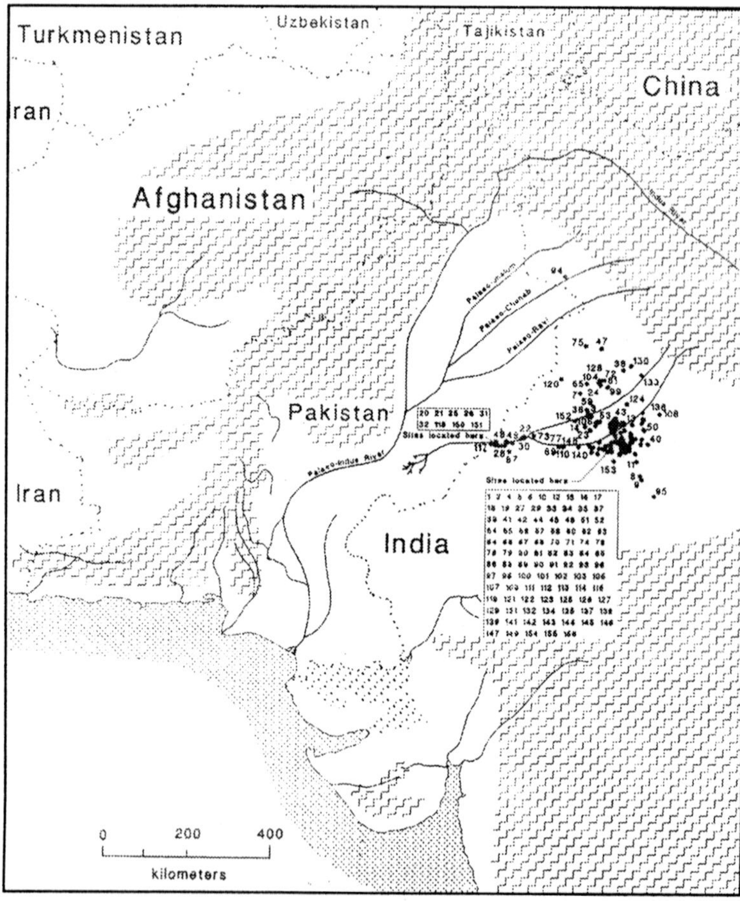

Fig. 8 : Map of sites of the Sothi-Siswal Phase after Possehl (2000)

The late Kot Diji: Kot Diji late phase is the transition phase of the early and mature Harappan and important sites of this phase are Kot Diji late deposit, Manda, Lewan, Tara Kai Quilla and Musakhel. The early Harappan transition stage preludes the mature Harappan civilization (Fig.9).

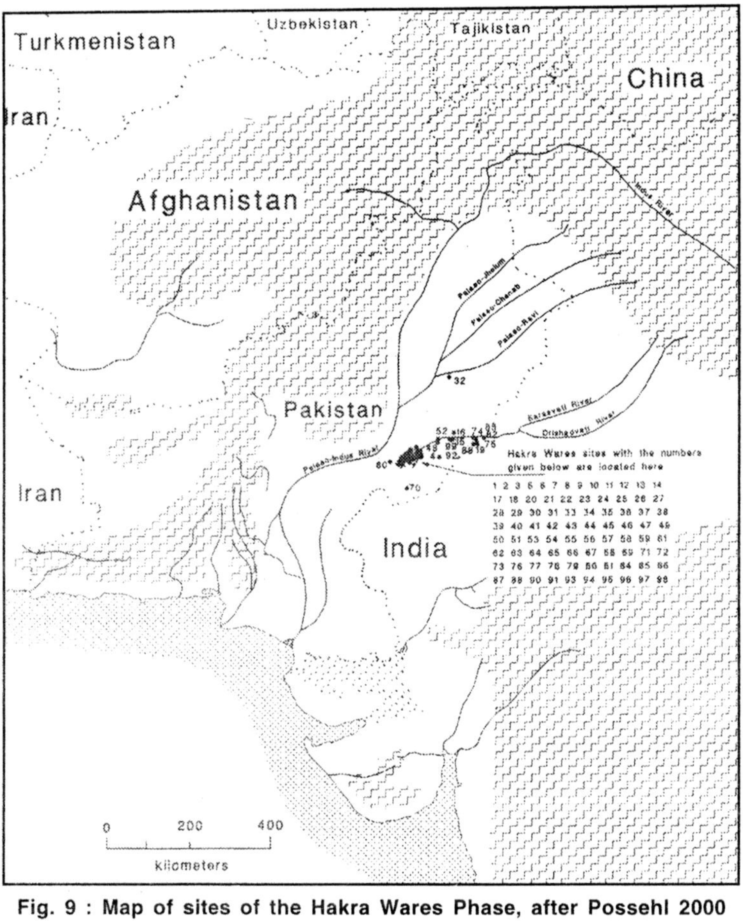

Fig. 9 : Map of sites of the Hakra Wares Phase, after Possehl 2000

Early Harappan Potteries site in India

Early Harappan Ceramics were also reported from Kunal, Banawali , Kalibangan, Rakhigarhi , Sothi, Siswal and Dhalewan-all located in north west India.

KUNAL

Kunal is Hakra ware and an early Harappan site in Hissar district of Haryana. The early ceramic of Kunal is Hakra ware which show the late tradition of Hakra ware of Cholistan. The pottery is red ware bearing painted designs in two colours: usually with a black outline filled in with white. The pottery of the late stage of Kunal is bichrome and the red ware painted motifs are peacock and pipal. Three radio carbon dates from Kunal lie between 3016 to 2577 B.C (Calibrated) (Fig.10).

Fig. 10 : Horned deity and trident on ceramic from Kunal 2800 B.C. Neg No. 2122-95, National Museum, New Delhi Collection

KALIBANGAN

Kalibangan is another early Harappan period site. The pottery from Kalibangan is red ware usually without any slip painted in two colours, namely, black and white. Thapar called this pottery as fabric A which is thick with thin bands on the upper part of body. Other category ceramics of the early Harappan period (other five) named from B to F. D type pottery is sturdy red ware basin with deeply incised designs on the interior part of the pottery. The pottery of category C are flanged rim jars, dishes and cups on stand. The C category pottery is made of fine grained clay carefully potted and well fired which had plum to red slip. The painted designs, usually executed in black pigment, included cross-hatched loops, fish-scales, filled in triangle, metopes, etc. Kalibangan early Harappan ceramics were also reported from Dhalewan, Rakhigarhi and Banawali (Fig.11).

Fig. 11 : Incised red ceramics, C. 2800-2700 B.C. (Early Harappan), Kalibangan

RAKHIGARHI

Rakhigarhi is another early Harappan site in Haryana. The Deposit of period I of Rakhigarhi is early Harappan type. The ceramic industry of Rakhigarhi shows all the six fabrics of Kalibangan including the technique of surface treatment, shapes and decorative elements. The pottery is identical with those of Banawali. It is light and thin in fabric, red to pinkish in colour and painted in black, combined at times with white, over a self-slipped dull surface. The geometric design on the pottery included horizontal bands, rows of latticed triangle, fish-scales, etc. The motifs used as filler were radiating lines ending in solid disks, four petalled flower, pipal leaf and a circle with radiating arches. The early Harappan shapes included the Jar with an out-turned rim; the basin and dish on stand are reported here. Some pieces of Hakra ware, reminiscent of Kunal pottery, were also discovered. The Hakra wares have already been reported from Kalibangan and Sothi. The main characteristics of Hakra ware type are (Fig.12) :

1. Incised
2. Applique
3. Dendrite, and
4. Ribbed or striated ware.

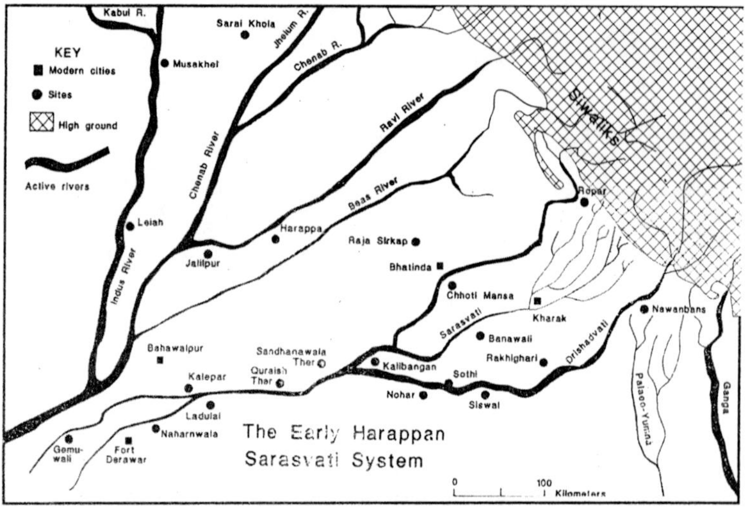

Fig. 12 : The Sarasvati River system during the Early Harappan Stage, modified from Wilhelmy 1969, after B.B.Lal, 1998

DHALEWAN

Dhalewan is an early Harappan site in Mansa district of East Punjab. The early Harappan ceramics of Dhalewan are red ware with black band, incised ware bichrome ware. Sothi is another early Harappan site in Rajasthan. The ceramics of Kalibangan A to F are reported from here.

2

The Harappan Civilization

During the third millennium B.C. (circa 2700-2000 B.C.) a highly developed civilization known as Harappan Civilization existed along the rivers Indus and Saraswati and Western Uttar Pradesh, all located in the north-Western part of South Asia. Charles Mason, who first saw the mound of Harappa in 1826, had hardly realized that the Harappa mound contained remains of the earliest civilization of South Asia. In 1862 Alexander Cunningham explored Harappa and found ceramics and seals. Later on, Major Clark also found a seal of a humpless bull from the same site. In 1917 the Italian scholar Lugi pio Tessitori had excavated Kalibangan but he could not publish his reports. Tessitori's Harappan material of 1917 excavation is now in the collection of State Museum, Bikaner . Tessitori explored some 85 sites and did excavations at Rang Mahal and Kalibangan. Nayanjot Lahiri recently studied Tessitori's collection now displayed in State Museum, Bikaner and confirmed that the material belongs to the Harappan age. Nothing of this Civilization was known until the early part of 20th century (1920-21) when two archaeologists,

R.D. Banerji and D.R. Sahani discovered Mohenjo-daro in Sindh and Harappa in Punjab, both now situated in Pakistan. During the last eight decades more than 2658 Early, Mature, Late Harappan and O.C.P. or Copper Hoard sites showing Harappan contacts have been discovered in the north west part of South Asia. Most of these newly discovered sites are in Saraswati Basin. So far 203 Harappan and its associated sites have been excavated. Mohenjo-daro, Harappa, Dholavira, Mehrgarh, Nausharo, Dhalewan, Kalibangan, Lothal, Nindawari, Chanhudaro, Rakhigarhi and Banawali have been extensively excavated. (Fig.13).

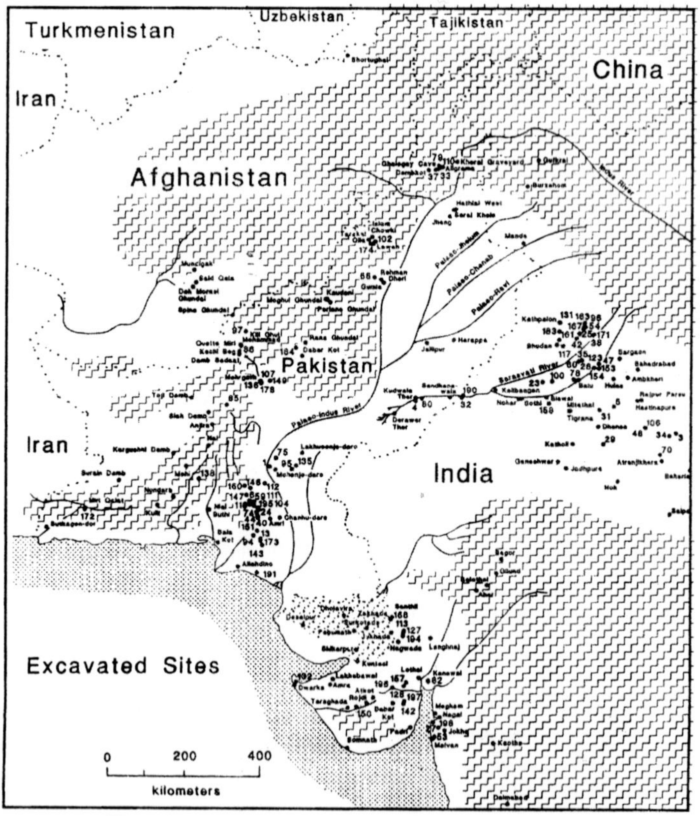

Fig. 13 : Excavated sites of the Harappan Age

NOMENCLATURE

The discovery of Harappan civilization was first made during 1920-22 in the Indus basin. In the succeeding decades after 1922 a large number of sites were discovered in the Indus Valley and Archaeologists named this as the Indus Civilization. This was due to the fact that the civilization was then limited to the Indus Valley proper. Some archaeologists have called it the Harappan Civilization named after Harappa, the first discovered site. The South Asian archaeologists have now come out with a new nomenclature, Indus-Saraswati Civilization or Saraswati (Hakra) Civilization.

EXTENT

The area covered (1.6 million sq.km) by the Harappan Civilization extended from Sutkagendor, on the Makran coast situated on the border of Iran and Pakistan, to Alamgirpur, Hulas, Mandi and Shamlinagar on the Hindon in western Uttar Pradesh, and from Shortaghai (Afghanistan) in the north to Daimabad in western Maharashtra. The extent of the Harappan Civilization in South Asia was greater in area than the contemporary civilization of the Nile in Egypt and the Euphrates and Tigris valley (Mesopotamia) in Syria and Iraq. The Ganweriwala, situated on the bank of river Saraswati (Hakra) is the largest mature Harappan site covering an area of 250 hectares. Rakhigarhi on the bank of river Drasdavati, a tributary of Saraswati and the Amrendra Nath excavator of Rakhigarhi had claimed its area to be 230 hectares. Another newly excavated site Dhalewan in Mansa district of Eastern Punjab (India) covers an area of 75 hectares. Mohenjo-daro and Dholavira are spread in 100 hectares. Harappa, situated on the bank of the river Ravi, covers 80 hectares, Mehrgarh Covers 200 hectares.

Lothal, Kuntasi, Cambay, Dwarika and Padri were small port towns of the Harappan period. The pattern of this civilization in certain respects was uniform as is evidenced not only from the seals, sealings, writings, beads, weights and measures, pottery, etc., but also from the bricks and brick-laying technique which are the same.

The early and Mature Harappan sites are located along the major rivers and, contrary to this, the late Harappan sites are found along the tributaries and in the upper reaches of the rivers. For convenience sake, the area of the Harappan civilization can now be divided into eight zones as follows :

1. Afghanistan (type site: Shortaghai)
2. Punjab (type sites: Harappa, Rohira and Dhalewan)
3. Rajasthan, Haryana (type sites: Kalibangan, Banawali and Rakhigarhi)
4. Bahawalpur (type site: Ganweriwala and Jalilpur)
5. Sindh (type site: Mohenjo-daro)
6. Baluchistan (type sites: Kulli Harappan phase and Nausharo)
7. Gujarat (type sites: Dholavira, Lothal, Rojdi, Kuntasi and Padri)
8. Western U. P. or upper Ganga-Yamuna Doab (type sites: Mandi, Hulas (Mandovali and Alamgirpur)

In India the Harappan sites are located on the eastern and southern periphery of the Harappan area. A few important excavated Harappan sites in the eastern region are Ropar, Dhalewan, Kalibangan, Mitathal, Siswal, Banawali, Rakhigarhi, Bhagwanpura, Manda, Hulas, Mandi and Rohira. The Harappan excavated sites of the southern region are Rangpur, Rojdi, Bhagatrav, Lothal, Bet-Dwarika, Daimabad, Dholavira, Kuntasi and Padri.

DATE

Pre-Harappan or Early Harappan is a formative stage of an antecedent village Chalcolithic Culture and this stage has been dated to circa 3500-2700 B.C. which preludes the later Mature Harappan urban civilization of South Asia. On the basis of calibrated radiocarbon dates the age of the Mature Harappan Civilization ranges from circa 2700 to 2000 B.C.The Late Harappan is a post mature Harappan village Chalcolithic Culture and this has been ascribed to circa 1900-1500 B.C.

Table : General Chronology of South Asia

Archaeological/ Historical Events	General Dates
Palaeolithic age	
Earliest stone tools (pebble)	+2MYA to 700,000
Lower Palaeolithic (Abbivillian Acheulian)	+1200,000- 300,000
Middle Palaeolithic (Mousterian)	300,000 to 40,000
Upper Palaeolithic	40,000 to 10,000
Epi-Palaeolithic	10,000 +/-1000
"Mesolithic" transition	10,000 to 6500 B.C.
Indus Valley Tradition Early Food Producing Era	
Neolithic/	ca. 8000 to 5000 B.C.
Chalcolithic	ca. 5000 to 3500 B.C.

(1)	(2)
Regionalization Era	
Early Harappan Phase	ca. 3500 to 2700 B.C.
Integration Era	
Harappan Phase	ca. 2700 to 2000 B.C.
Localization Era	
Late Harappan Phase	ca. 1900 to 1500 B.C.
Post-Indus or Indo-Gangetic Tradition Regionalization Era	
Copperhoard Culture	ca. 2800 to 1500 B.C.
Iron age	ca. 2000-600 B.C.
Painted Grey Ware	ca. 1600 to 700 B.C.
Northern Black Polished Ware	ca. 700 to 100 B.C.
Early Historic Period begins around 600 B.C.	
Buddha (Siddhartha Gautama)	563-483 B.C. (or 440-360 B.C.)
Panini (Sanskrit Grammarian)	ca. 500-400 B.C.
Alexander of Macedon receives "submission" and becomes the "ally" of Ambhi, King of Taxila, 326 B.C.	
Integration Era	
Mauryan Empire	ca 317-185 B.C.
Chandragupta Maurya	ca. 317-298 B.C.
Kautilya (Minister of Chandragupta, probable author of Arthashastra)	ca. 317-298 B.C.
Bindusara	ca. 298-274 B.C.
Ashoka	ca. 274-232 B.C.

Period	Date range	Site	14c date (B.C.)	Calibrated date (B.C.)
EARLY	2900-3300 B.C.	HARAPPA	2725± 185	
			2725± 90	3338, 3213
		MOHENJO-DARO	?	——
		MEHRGARH IV	2365± 145	2877,2708
		REHMAN DEHRI II	2705± 115	3226,3147
		JODHPURA (GANESHWAR)		
		KALIBANGAN, I	2370± 120	2879,2709
		KUNAL I		3000
		SURKOTADA IA	2515± 135	2865,2668
MATURE	2900-1900 B.C.	HARAPPA	2470± 70	2913
		MOHENJO-DARO	2155± 65	2556
		(Middle/Late)		2493
		SHORTUGAI I	2245± 100	2651,2610
		LOTHAL IIIB	2080± 133	2461
		I A		2800
		PRABHAS PATAN	1755± 95	1955
		KALIBANGAN II	2225± 115	2586
		BANAWALI		
LATE	1900-1500 B.C.	LOTHAL Va	1555± 130	1735,1701
				to
		LOTHAL Vc	——	1600
		DAIMABAD	1760± ?	1961
		ROJDI	1285± ?	1424
		BET-DWARKA	1528 (TL)	1528

Fig. 18A Chronological bracket based on 14C of Harappan site after S.R. Rao (2001).

ORIGIN

A few Harappan sites show continuous sequence i.e. Early Mature and Late Harappan. Such sites are Harappa, Nausharo, Dholavira, Banawali, Rakhigarhi, Kalibangan and Dhalewan (Fig. 14).

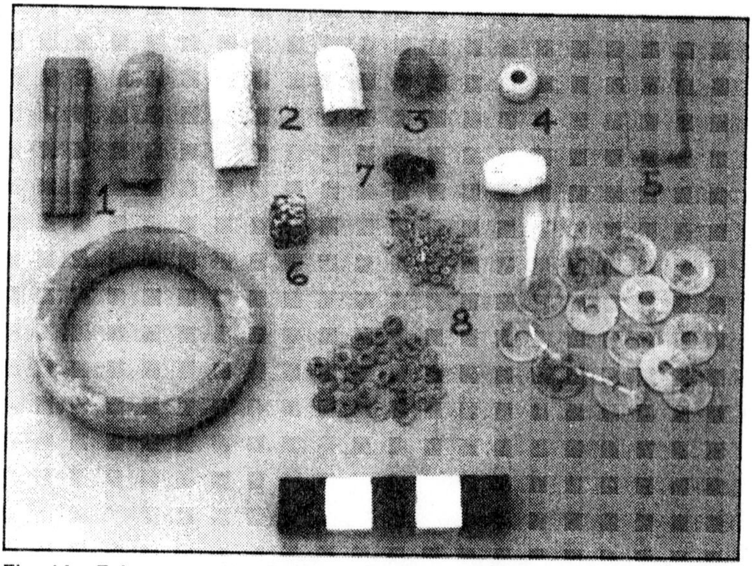

Fig. 14 : Faience steatite Bangles, Steatite & Lapislazuli beads, C. 2800-2700 B.C. Early Mature transition Dhalewan, Loan from A.S.I. National Museum, New Delhi Collection

The latest evidence from the sites such as Dhalewan, Harappa early deposit (Ravi phase), Banawali, Kunal, Rakhigarhi, Dholavira, Nausharo, Mehrgarh, Lewan, Sothi, Sherikhan Tarkai, Rehmandheri, Amri, Ghazishah and Kotdiji shows the independent growth of Harappan culture from circa 8000 to 2000 B.C. The transitional phase between Early Harappan village Chalcolithic and the Mature Urban Harappan has been reported from Banawali, Dholavira, Padri, Dhalewan, Kunal and Nausharo. The author (D.P. Sharma) has dated the transitional phase between circa 2800-2700 B.C. The transitional phase material from Kunal is most interesting where two crowns, armlets, bangles, a necklace and pendants of various sizes in precious metals (gold and silver); 12000 beads of Carnelian; and seven Steatite Seals having Mature Harappan square shape with boss at back but without the typical animal and pictographic script have been found.

On the basis of the archaeological finds from the Early Harappan sites we can say that the Early Harappans had the knowledge of dish-on-stand shaped pots and were also acquainted with the fish scale, *swastika* symbol and pipal leaf design on pottery. They had knowledge of distant trade contact. The Horn design and pipal leaf are well depicted on the ceramics of Early Harappan Period (Fig. 15). The concept of the square seals without script was there. The Early Harappan seals were made of clay, bone and ivory. At Kunal seven steatite seals of the early Harappan age have been found. These have a geometric motif and an incipient boss on the back. Microblades of chalcedony were also reported from Kunal. Triangular terracotta cakes, dices and chert blades are also available in the Early Harappan level. Some graffiti marks found on the artifacts at the early Harappan sites like Harappa, etc., are akin to those of Mature Harappan. The Graffiti marks are an integral part of the Mature Harappan Civilization. The Harappan revolution took place in the region of Mehrgarh, Kotdiji,

Fig. 15 : Horned deity depiction on pot, C. 2700 B.C. Burzhom National Museum New Delhi Collection

Harappa, Dhalewan, Rehmandheri, Cambay, Anartha (Gujarat) and Kunal, around circa 2700-2600 B.C. (Fig. 16)

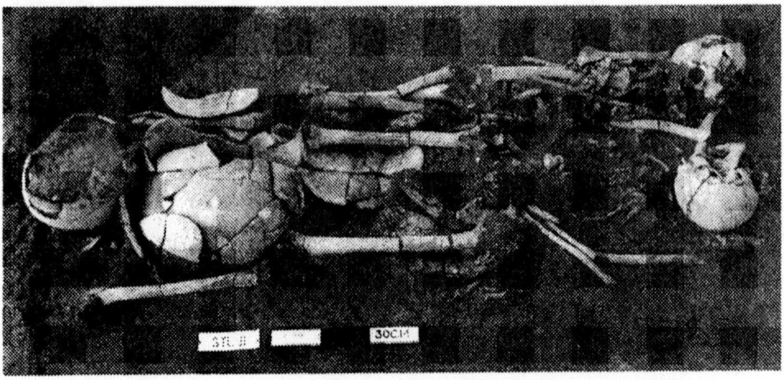

Fig. 16 : Early Harappan Burials Pottery from Nagwada, M.S. University Baroda Collection

MIGRATION

The Early Harappans first made their settlement around 3500 B.C. in Baluchistan. Later on they shifted to Harappa and Mohenjo-daro and developed themselves further and became Mature Harappans. Harappa and Mohenjo-daro are the nucleus regions of Mature Harappans. J. P. Joshi recently suggested that from Sindh, the Harappans migrated eastward and made the fortified cities at Kotara near Kuran and Khavada. Later on they crossed a strip of Rann of Kutch at Amarakpur and again made a big Harappan fortified city at Dholavira. The Harappans came via Allahdino and Kotara to Dholavira. Later on they made a citadel at Surkotada. They also made their settlements at Lothal, Kuntasi and Padri. After the end of the Mature Harappan period they moved to Western Maharashtra. Through Hakra-Saraswati (Gaggar) region they came to Kalibangan, Dhalewan in Eastern Punjab, Banawali and Rakhigarhi in Haryana. Around circa 2000 B.C they moved to the region of upper Ganga-Yamuna Doab in western U. P. and made their Harappan settlements at Alamgirpur, Hulas, Mandi, Mandavali and Nayabans on the banks of river Hindon and the Yamuna. In the last they mixed with the local cultures of western U. P. Ahar, Balathal and Oziyana, all village Chalcolithic Culture sites of Rajasthan and adjoining region of western Madhya Pradesh. On the basis of C14 dating Ahar village Chalcolithic Culture has been dated between circa 3100 and 1500 B.C. We can correlate the early Ahar material culture with the Vedic culture (Rigveda, Yajurvaveda, Samaveda and Atharvaveda). The Early Vedic people were contemporary with the Early Harappan. The Mature Harappans were having contacts with the Samavedic and Atharvavedic people. The Late Harappans were contemporary with the late Ahar or later Vedic culture. The copper hoard culture of western group was contemporary with the Mature and late Harappan. The Copper hoard period begins around circa 2800 B.C. and ends in 1500 B.C. One thing is very clear that the Harappan Civilization was not Rigvedic but it shows contacts with the Atharvavedic Aryans of the Vedic age.

HARAPPAN COLLECTION IN THE NATIONAL MUSEUM

The National Museum, New Delhi, has in its pride possession a collection of around 3800 artifacts collected from various sites like Mohenjo-daro, Harappa, Chanhudaro, Amri and Nal, all situated in the Indus Valley region of Pakistan, apart from 1000 objects from Indian Harappan sites recently received from the Archaeological Survey of India, New Delhi on temporary loan. The new material is from the sites of Dholavira, Dhalewan, Kalibangan, Banawali, Lothal, Sothi, Rakhigarhi, Mandi, Hulas, Alamgirpur, Ropar, Bhagwanpur and Burzahom (Fig.17). This new permanent gallery is a Joint Project of the Archaeological Survey of India and the National Museum, New Delhi. Many questions remain

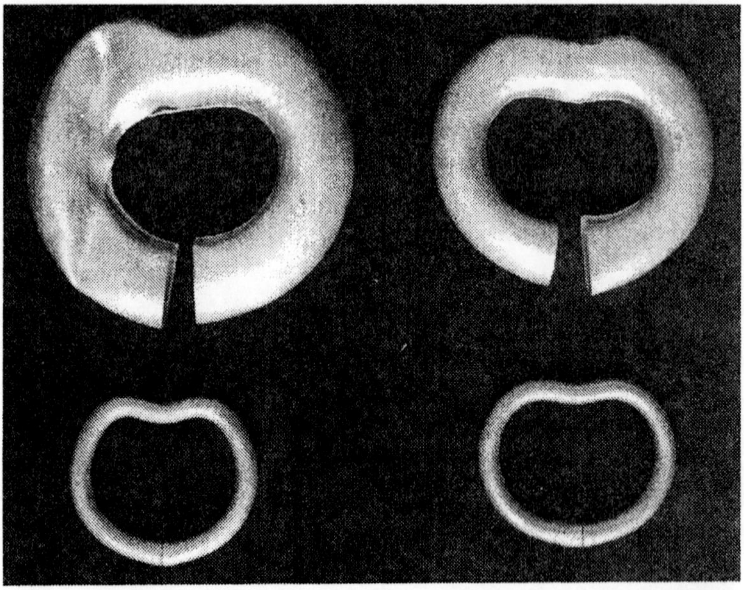

Fig. 17 : Kara (Bracelet) Gold, Solid Hollow-Mandi, District Mujaffarnagar, C. 2000-1900 B.C. Mature-Late Harappan Transition, National Museum New Delhi Collection (Loan from A.S.I.)

unanswered about this civilization. No one is very sure about the mysterious written record and some scholars have recently suggested that the Indus script is on the way to its final decipherment. The archaeologists have found a number of clues, and the research and serious study of the great civilization continues with greater enthusiasm till date. With these objects and the photographs of the archaeological remains, this Harappan gallery presents a picture of how things might have been during the development of the Harappan Bronze Age Civilization. The Archaeological Survey of India and the National Museum have jointly set up a new permanent Harappan Gallery, for the visitors in the very first year of this new century. The material on display has been selected carefully to make the gallery more exciting, charming and meaningful from the educational point of view and the new publications like *Terracotta Art* and *Script of the Harappan Civilization* will be an added attraction. We are going to introduce multimedia in the Harappan Gallery of the National Museum, New Delhi.

IMPORTANT FEATURES

In the well-planned town area of the Harappans we find wide straight streets and major roads running north-south and east west and cutting each other at right angles with covered drains running along the sides (Fig.18). Most of these towns were divided into two parts and were fortified with high walls made of bricks or stones (Fig.19).

Fig. 18 : Main street of Dholavira mature Harappan period (C. 2600-2000 B.C.) after Bisht 2001

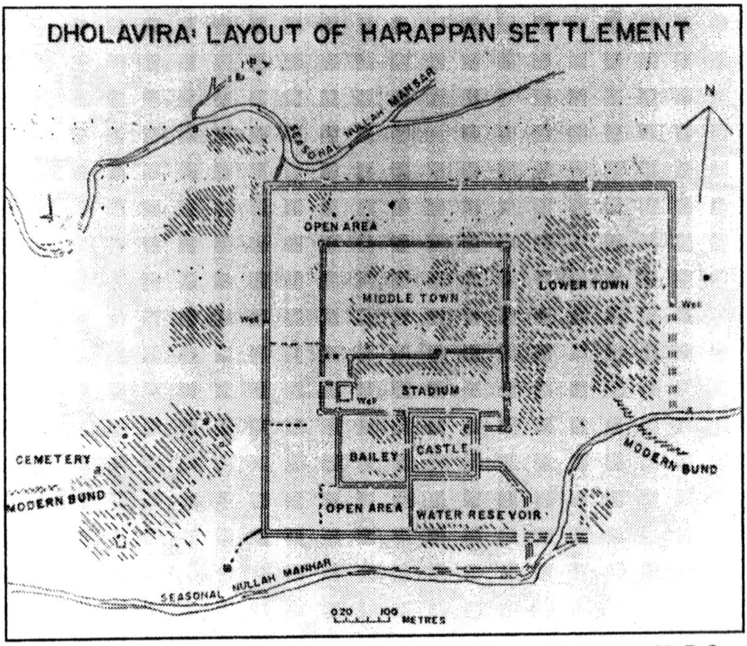

Fig. 19 : Dholavira layout of Harappan Settlement C. 2600-2000 B.C. photograph after R.S. Bisht : 2000 Neg No. 441-2000 (N.N.)

The Major town found at Dholavira has three parts, and these three architectural components were enclosed by an outer fortification wall. The rock-cut reservoir discovered at Dholavira suggests a unique water management system at this Harappan site (Fig.20). Rakhigarhi was the largest animal husbandry and crafts centre located on the eastern periphery of the Harappan civilization discovered so far. Mandi in western U.P. seems to be a Goldsmith workshop or store house of the Harappans who had migrated from the West in 2000 B.C. (Fig. 21).

The Harappan houses were built mostly of bricks and stone on high platforms. They had stairs, bathrooms and a well-laid drainage system both covered and open. The pots used were made of baked clay and the people lived in a

Fig. 20 : Reservoir (Tank) from Dholavira. Mature Harappan period after R.S. Bisht, 2001

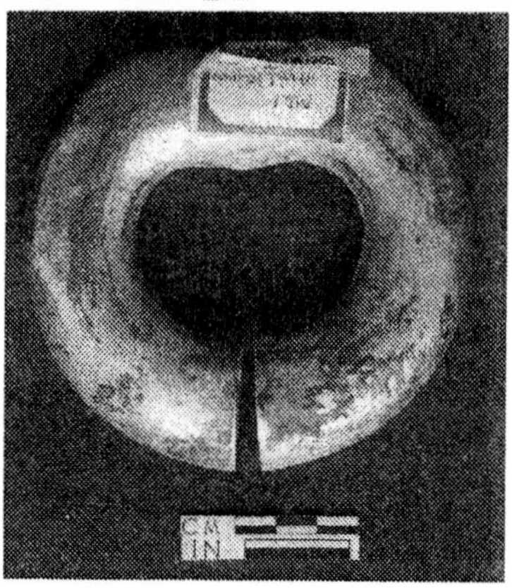

Fig. 21 : Silver Jewellery from Mandi, Mature Late Harappan Transition

prosperous style as is evident from the gold jewellery, clay and stone toys, terracottas, seals and a variety of figurines of faience and paste. They farmed the land with ploughs near the settlements and grew plenty of wheat, barley, cotton, millet and crops besides date, sesame and melon. They ploughed agricultural fields, and terracotta models of plough have been discovered from Kalibangan and Banawali.

SETTLEMENT PATTERNS

The Mature Harappan settlements were mostly located on the banks of the rivers Indus, Saraswati and their tributaries. According to J. P. Joshi, the *"Harappans were conditioned by the behaviour of the river providing an active flood plain and ecology, navigability of the river, accessibility to natural resources and trade routes both internal and external. Development of Harappan urban centre is mostly dependent on these factors"*. (Joshi, 2001)

The Harappan settlements are built of mud bricks, burnt bricks and chiselled stones. They also used wood for the doors. The use of bricks was limited at Dholavira, Rojdi and Surkotada, all Mature Harappan sites in Gujarat (Fig.22). The ratio of Mature Harappan brick size is 1: 2 : 4. The Mature Harappans executed their town planning with geometric instruments which and they had developed i.e. the compass, the plumb bob and the right angle measuring instruments, etc. These instruments gave them accuracy in town planning and building streets. These measuring instruments were found at Lothal, Dholavira, Mohenjo-daro, Kalibangan and Allahdino (Fig.23a-c). The right angle measuring instruments were found at Dholavira, Lothal and Mohenjo-daro. The linear measuring scales have been found at Lothal, Kalibangan, Mohenjo-daro and Allahdino.

Fig. 22 : Northern Gateway of the Citadel, Dholavira after R.S. Bisht 1998.

Fig. 23 :

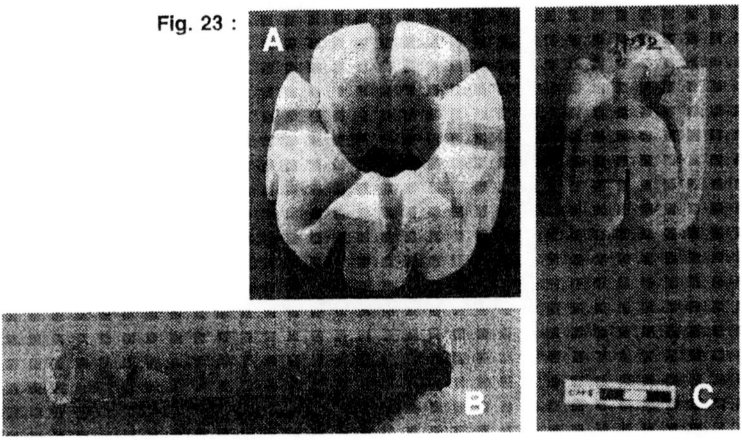

Fig. 23a : Angle Measuring Instrument shell C. 2600 B.C. Mohenjodaro, National Museum, Karachi Collection.

Fig. 23b : Linear measuring scale, C. 2600 B.C. Kalibangan, Terracotta, A.S.I. New Delhi Collection.

Fig. 23c : Compass right angle measuring instrument shell. C. 2600-2000 B.C. Acc. No. 2751 Neg No. LM/1797733, 94-95. Loan from A.S.I. National Museum, New Delhi Collection.

Mature Harappan sites like Harappa, Mohenjo-daro and Kalibangan had each a citadel on high mound in the west and a fortified chessboard pattern lower town in the east. The Harappan citadels have gateways with flights of steps to climb up to the platforms. The citadel is divided into two parts i.e. one having platforms and the other having a residential complex for the elite, separated by a wall. (Fig. 24).

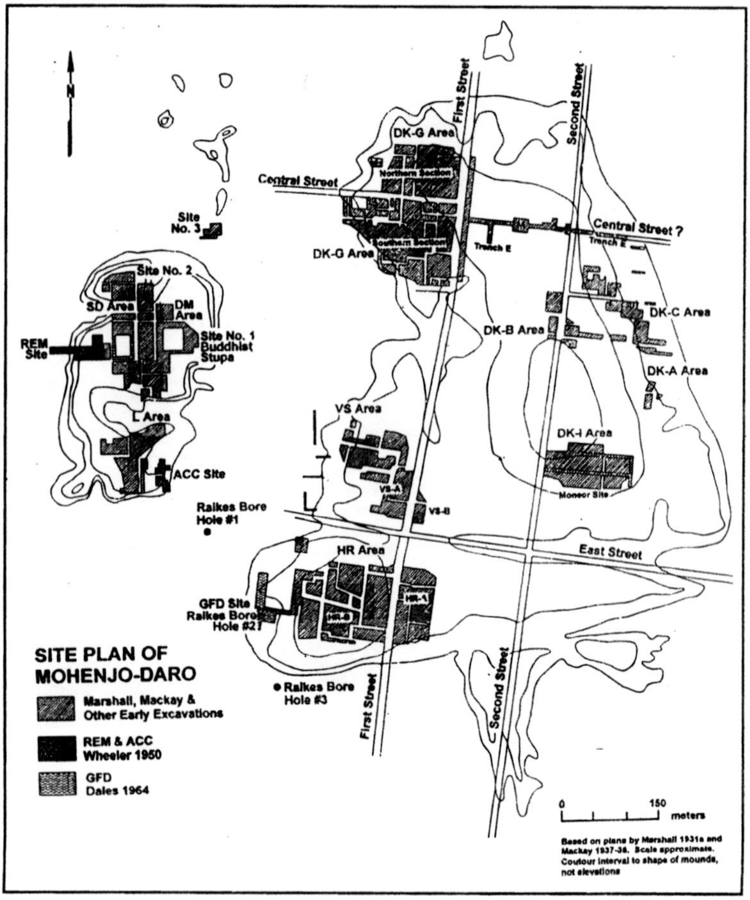

Fig. 24 : Plan of Mohenjo-daro after Jansen

The Lothal port town had a dockyard, a warehouse, a granary, a high acropolis and a lower town (Fig.25). The stone town planning of Surkotada differs from that of Kalibangan. Surkotada had a citadel and a fortified lower residential town. These two divisions were surrounded by a rectangular fortification wall made of stone rubbles. The fortification wall had an imposing gateway. The citadel and the lower town had interred communication ramp and

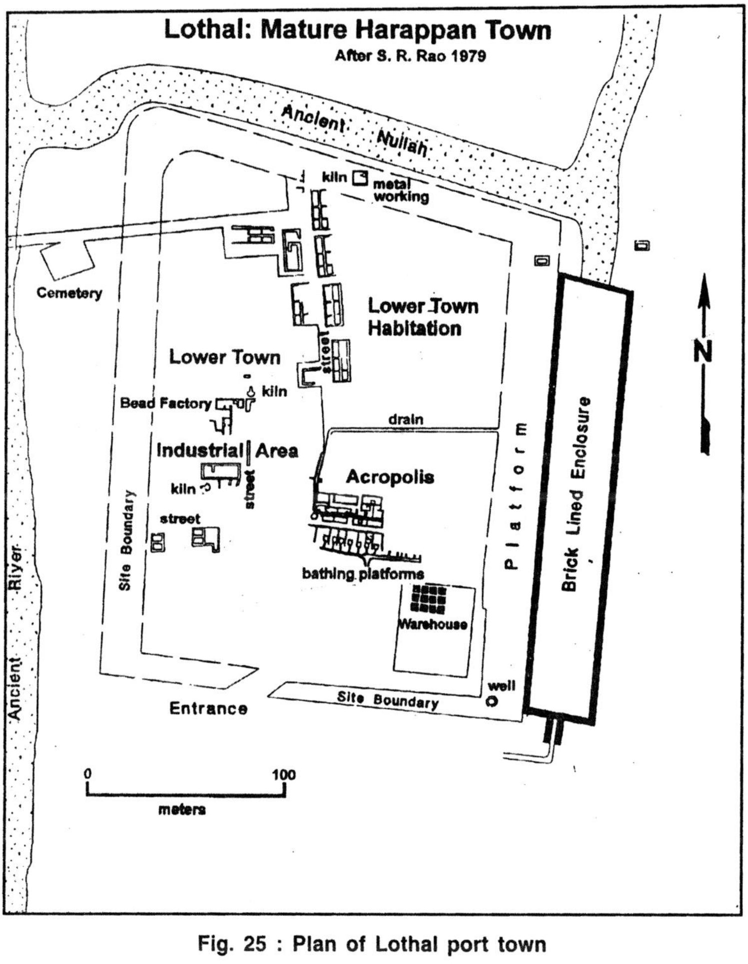

Fig. 25 : Plan of Lothal port town

gateways (Fig.26). Stone architecture was also discovered at Rojdi. The houses were built of stone rubbles. Kuntasi in Gujarat was a centre for procuring raw material and processing them into finished products. It was another Harappan port town for exporting items to West Asia.

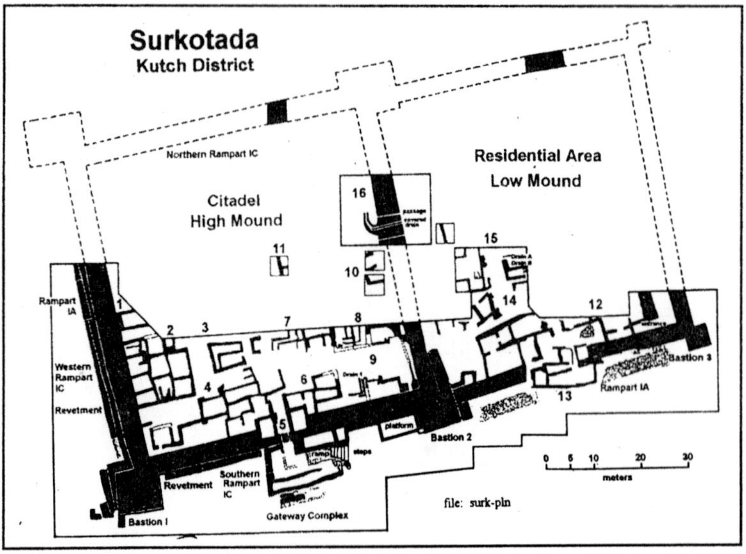

Fig. 26 : Plan of Surkotada with the fortifications after J.P. Joshi 1994

The Dholavira town planning had three principal divisions named as Acropolis (Citadel), middle town and lower town, which was surrounded by a rectangular massive stone fortification wall. The entire Harappan walled city occupied an area of nearly 100 h. The Citadel was provided with one gate at each side. The highly polished stone blocks and pillars used in the passage and the architectural components were without parallel at any other Mature Harappan site discovered so far (Fig.27). Around the Citadel there are almost 13m wide water reservoirs along with a feeder channel covered with slabs and provided with man holes for occasional desilting. So far around 18 reservoirs and one stadium have been reported from Dholavira (Fig. 28). The most outstanding discovery is the find of a large-sized signboard inscription of ten

Fig. 27 : Stone building, C. 2600 B.C. Dholavira after Bisht 1994

Fig. 28 : Conjectual view of water reservoir at Dholavira. Photograph after R.S. Bisht 2001.

Harappan signs (Fig.29). The town planning of Banawali shows minor differences from that of Kalibangan and Mohenjo-daro. The Banawali Citadel and lower town was secured by a mud brick fortification on three sides and was designed like an irregular trapezium following the planning of the Early Harappans with a few marginal modifications in the lay-out. During the late Mature Harappan period the people of Banawali dug a deep and broad moat around the town. The Lower town and the citadel were set within a single compound of semi-circular shape. The street systems of Banawali are of radial type (Fig. 30).

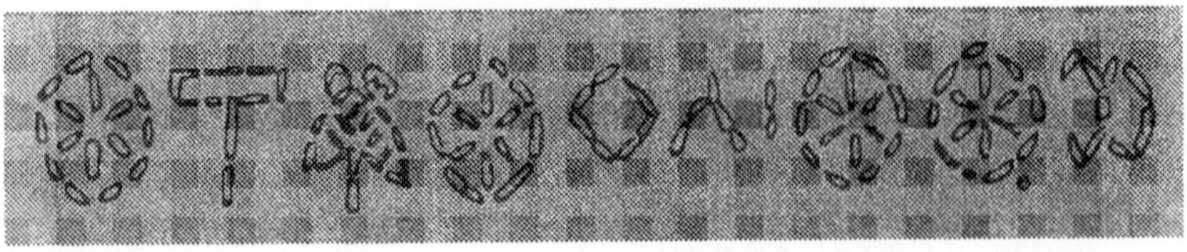

Fig. 29 : Sign board inscription from Dholavira after Bisht 2001.

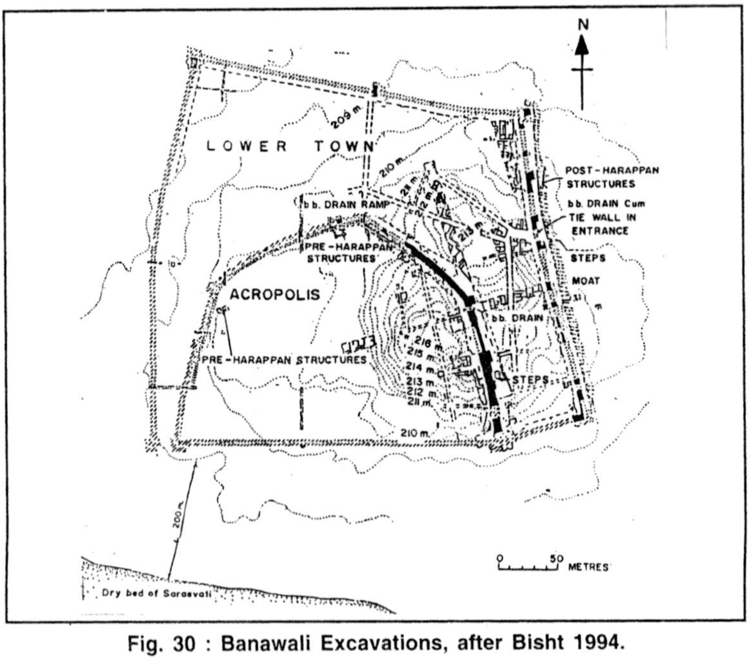

Fig. 30 : Banawali Excavations, after Bisht 1994.

The town planning of the newly excavated Harappan sites like Rakhigarhi (Haryana) and Dhalewan (Punjab) is identical with that of Kalibangan. The mud brick architecture of these sites reminds one of the typical Mature Harappan Style. Rakhigarhi seems to be a Mature Harappan animal husbandry centre and Dhalewan represents a transitional stage between the Early and Mature Harappans. Further extensive horizontal excavations on these sites will provide the final answer to the settlement pattern.

SETTLEMENT PATTERN IN GHAGGAR-SARASWATI (HAKRA) REGIONS

Hakra or Ghaggar or Saraswati river with its tributaries was a mighty river during the chalcolithic Early and Mature Harappan period (circa 5000-2000 B.C.). A large number (around 1048) of Harappan and its associated sites lie in this region. This river system provided better communication in Haryana, East Punjab, Bahawalpur and the Kutch regions for getting timber (wood) from Himachal Pradesh, which was used as building material by the Harappans. The largest Harappan settlements like Mohenjo-daro, Harappa, Ganweriwala, Dholavira, Rakhigarhi, etc., are located along the major and perennial rivers (Fig. 31).

The Kutch regions of Harappan mounds are larger and have a thicker habitation deposit. This area is located in *lower* Saraswati (Hakra) region where it joins the Arabian sea near Desalpur in Kutch.

J.P. Joshi called these areas of Saraswati region as the foundation of urban boom. A recent discovery of circa 7000-2700 B.C. old under water settlement, at cambay on the Gujarat coast support J.P. Joshi's theory. However, the present author differs from him because this region is located in the peripheral region of Harappan Civilization. Its nucleus region is Mohenjo-daro and Harappa where

Fig. 31 : Major sites of the Indus-Saraswati civilization after S.P. Gupta 1997

the urban phase begins circa 2700-2600 B.C. The recent excavations done by Kenoyer at Harappa have confirmed the existence of circa 3500-3300 B.C. old earliest deposit of Ravi culture which preludes the early Harappans and Harappan cultures. It contradicts the observation made by J.P. Joshi. The sites like Mehrgarh, Nausharo, Rehmandheri, etc., show a continuous evolution from circa 8000-7000 B.C. to circa 2700 B.C. and this suggests that the Harappan Civilization had its origin in Mehrgarh region (Fig.32).

SOCIAL STRATIFICATION

On the basis of the settlement pattern of the Mature Harappan sites J. P. Joshi and B. B. Lal have suggested that

"The Mature Harappan seems to be divided into three classes: one elite associated with the population of citadel (Acropolis), a well-to-do middle class occupying the lower town, and a relatively weaker section working for the upper and middle class". The separate quarters for workmen found at mature Harappan sites suggest the prevalent social stratification. On the basis of the available archaeological evidences it has been observed, *"That the Harappan habitation pattern was not based solely on the economic status of people but on the basis of the power status of the ruling class including the priestly one".*

Fig. 32 : Large mud brick structure of stone Mehrgarh Pd. II C. 5500-4800 B.C. after B.B. Lal 1998.

On the basis of two divisions of town planning i.e. citadel and lower town, we can conclude that the religious elite population had occupied the citadel area of the mature Harappan town. The wealthy traders, occupational class and the poor section i.e. workers, etc., lived in the lower town. The citadel had more civic amenities than the lower town. The archaeological evidence from Lothal and Dholavira suggests that the entire Mature Harappan trade and marketing was done from the lower town.

BUILDINGS

The houses were built of bricks and stones along the roads. Every house contained several rooms, a kitchen, a well and a bathroom around the courtyard. The drainage system was perfect. The house drains emptied all the wastewater into the street drains (Fig. 33).

Fig. 33 : Lothal drain & Soakege pits C. 2500-2000 B.C. Photograph after S.R. Rao : 1991

The Great Bath at Mohenjo-daro shows the state of perfection reached in the perfect building techniques. The fired bricks were held together by *chuna* mortar and Asphalt to make them watertight. The water could be drained out by an opening in one corner. The Great Bath was surrounded by a cloister, into which opened a number of small rooms. It is 39 x 23 feet in area and 8 feet in depth (Fig.34). Eighteen rock-cut reservoirs and stone buildings have been discovered at Dholavira, a mature Harappan site in India. These reservoirs were used for storing water.

WHO WERE THE HARAPPANS?

The Harappans belonged to a homogeneous race. The latest evidence from the excavated sites now indicates the close affinity between the Mature Harappan settlement pattern as reported from Rakhigarhi, Banawali, Lothal, Kalibangan and Dholavira and that of the early Aryans. The burial practices and *Lingayat* cult associate the

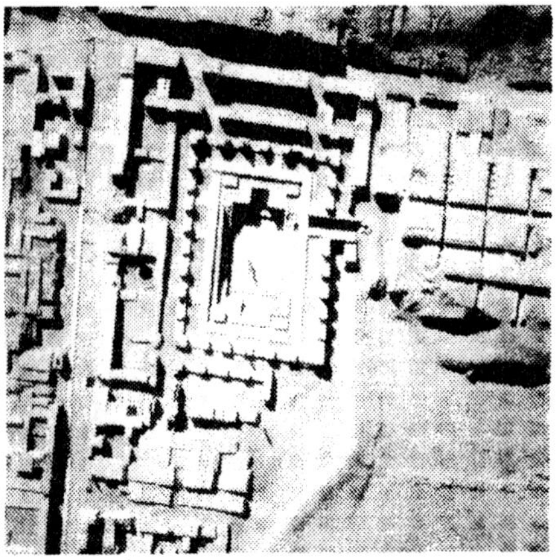

Fig. 34 : Great bath made of burnt bricks. C. 2700-2000 B.C. Mohenjodaro Neg No. 2-2000 (N.M.)

Harappans with the proto-Dravidians of South Asia. The Harappans were mostly a mixed population of Aryans and proto-Dravidians. Bhagwan Singh has suggested their affinity with the Vedic Aryans. However, the author (D.P. Sharma) feels that the Mature Harappans were very different from the Rigvedic people and they may be contemporary of the *Atharvavedic and Samavedic* Aryans who were not urban like the mature Harappans.

J. P. Joshi has observed that the Ghaggar-Saraswati (Hakra) river system had three major economic pockets. The first pocket was on the north along the Sirhind river, a tributary of Ghaggar having an area of 120 km in Mansa district, Punjab, where seven very big mounds, six middle mounds and five small mounds associated with the Harappan period have been discovered. The commercial interaction is indicative of a Harappan Civilization. Dhalewan, an Early and Mature-Harappan site, is located in this region and this site shows a transitional stage between Early and Mature Harappans. Kunal, Rakhigarhi and Banawali fall nearby the first region.

The second Harappan pocket was in Bikaner-Bahawalpur of Ghaggar region, where around 800

Harappans and its associated sites have been discovered in an area of 1000 km. It includes the area from Yazdan to Derawar fort belonging to the Early and Mature Harappan sites and other sites which have Harappan influence. Ganweriwala, the largest Mature Harappan site, covering an area of 250 hectares is located in this region. The third southern area is in Kutch, which is half way between Sindh and Gujarat. It has a concentration of 100 Harappan sites and the area of Dholavira and Surkotada are located in this region. Dholavira was spread in a 100-hectare area. J. P. Joshi is of the opinion: "*These three economic pockets in the cultural empire of the Harappan provided a strong economic base that is the foundation of the Harappan boom*".

The River Hindon of western U. P. or upper Ganga-Yamuna Doab was also a tributary of the river Yamuna and around 200 Harappan and its associated sites have been located in the Hindon system. According to the present author (D.P. Sharma) Rigvedic and Yajurvedic cultures are contemporary of the Early Harappan village Chalcolithic Culture. We need some more archaeological evidence to show the close affinity between Rigvedic, Aryans and Mature Harappans. The discovery of horse bones and terracotta, fire altars and copper hoard from the Mature Harappan sites simply shows that the Mature Harappans and the Atharvavedic (Author of copper hoard) had come in contact with each other but they were not the same (Fig.35). The recent findings of a

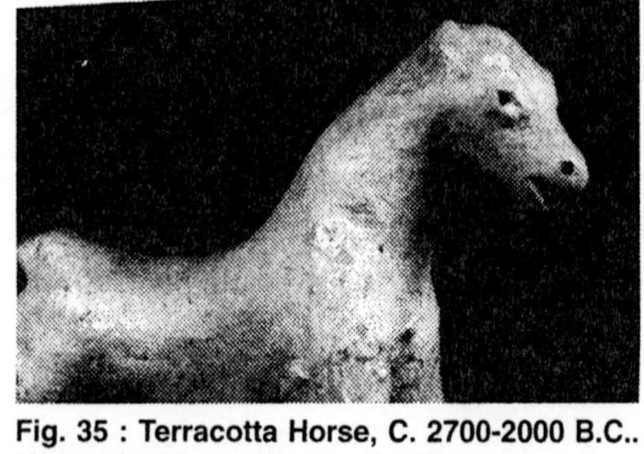

Fig. 35 : Terracotta Horse, C. 2700-2000 B.C.. Mohenjodaro, National Museum, New Delhi Collection. Neg. No. R1667 (N.M.)

terracotta figurine of a cow from Oziayana and the non-Harappan Chalcolithic material from Balathal (which has been ascribed to circa 3100-2500 B. C.) show affinity with the Yajurvavedic and Rigvedic village Chalcolithic Culture. Rigvedic is not post-Mature Harappan and its period can be pushed back to the contemporary Early Harappan Period (circa 3500-2700 B.C.).

FIGURINES AND TOYS

The most beautiful of all the figurines found at Mohenjo-daro are two small figures of a dancing girl in bronze (Fig. 36-37). The other rare bronze figurines are

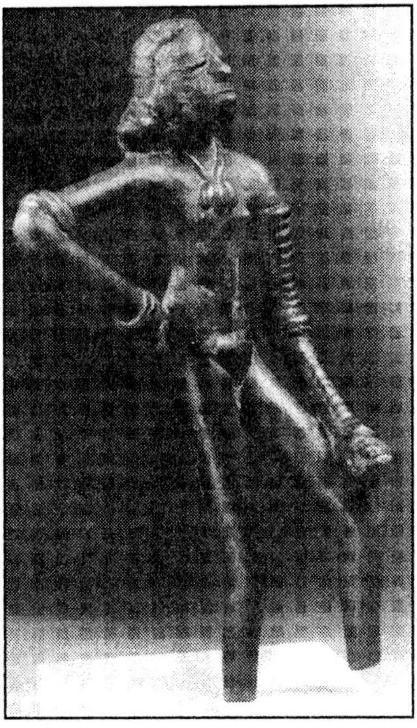

Fig. 36 : Side View Dancing girl. C. 2700 B.C. Mohenjodaro, Copper National Museum, New Delhi, after Jansen, 2000.

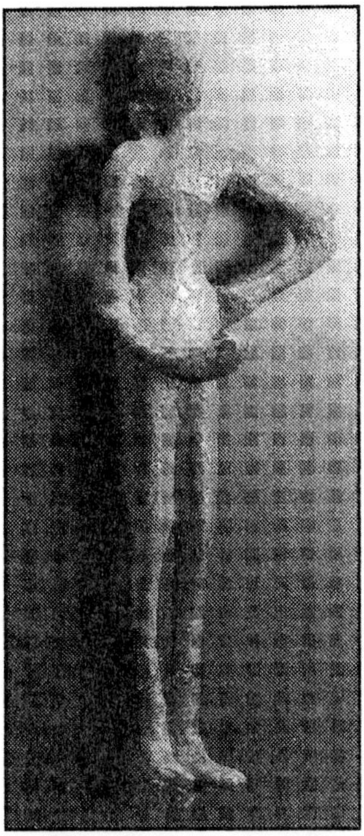

Fig. 37 : Dancing Girl C. 2700 B.C. Mohenjodaro, Copper, National Museum, Karachi Collection.

buffaloes from Mohenjo-daro and a bull from Kalibangan. This and other figurines of men, women, animals, birds and toys were solid cast in bronze by the lost wax or *cire-perdue* method. There is a finely crafted small buffalo and a model of a cart with wheels. There are also bronze mirrors, hairpins and utencils and pans. The other huge bronze images of the late mature Harappan period (2000 B.C.) are one chariot and three animals from Daimabad (Fig. 38). The most interesting is a terracotta toy animal with a head that moves. There is also a bird on wheels, a climbing monkey, a horse, a maze and a bull-all models of clay (Fig. 39). The rare terracotta figurines of a male head, an inscribed double male head, an unhumped bull and a charging bull from Kalibangan are of unique artistic

Fig. 38 : Animal image. C. 2000 B.C. Copper, Daimabad National Museum Collection, New Delhi

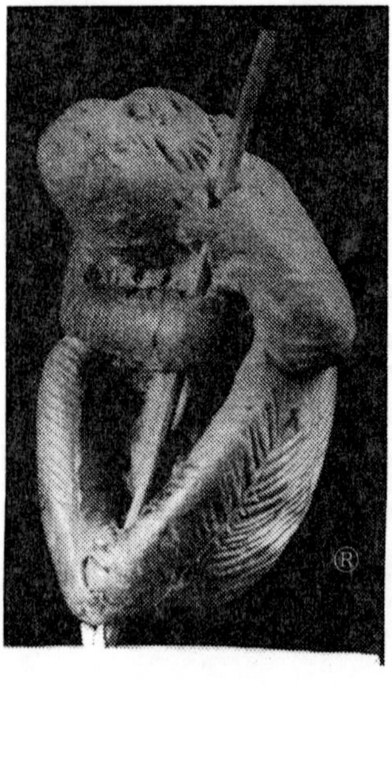

Fig. 39 : Climbing monkey of clay. 2500 B.C. Mohenjodaro Acc No. BK 1625/216. Neg. No. P.H. 81-7-712. National Museum New Delhi Collection.

value. There are a large number of terracotta figurines from Mohenjo-daro, Harappa, Banawali, Chanhudaro, Lothal, Nausharo, Rakhigarhi, Kalibangan and Dholavira. Among these are figures of mother goddesses, birds, water and land animals. The famous stone bust of a bearded man, clad in embroidered shawl with trefoil motif, now in the National Museum, Karachi, resembles the image of a priest. Its plaster cast copy is on display in the National Museum, New Delhi. A similar type of a headless priest seated in stone and mongooses have been recently reported from Dholavira. A male torso and a dancer made of jasper stone from Harappa and a Male steatite head from Mohenjo-daro now on display in the National Museum, New Delhi, are other unique examples of stone art (Fig. 40).

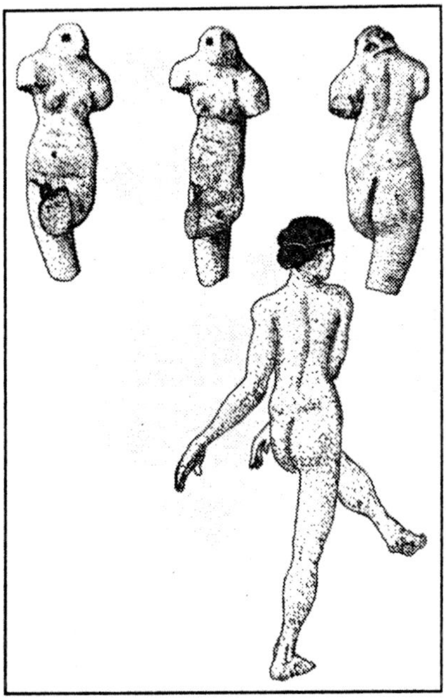

Fig. 40 : Twisted figure of female dancer, grey sand stone, Harappa, Consectual sketches of dancer from Harappa after Marshall 1931 Fig. Kenoyer : 1998 : 129.

JEWELLERY

The craftsmen in the cities of this period worked with gold, silver, copper, bronze, shell, paste, ivory, faience and clay to produce all kinds of ornaments (Fig. 41). They made beads out of semi-precious stones, shells, ivory and clay. They used gold and silver to make bracelets, necklaces, bangles, earrings, head ornaments and girdles. The earliest jewellery items of gold and silver in South Asia have been recently reported from Kunal, Nindawari and Nagawada and these have been ascribed to c. 3100-2800 B.C. (Early Harappan period) The gold jewellery of the Mature Harappan period was reported from Mandi, Mohenjo-daro, Nindawari, Allahdino, Rakhigarhi, Lothal, Quetta, Dholavira and Harappa (Fig. 42).

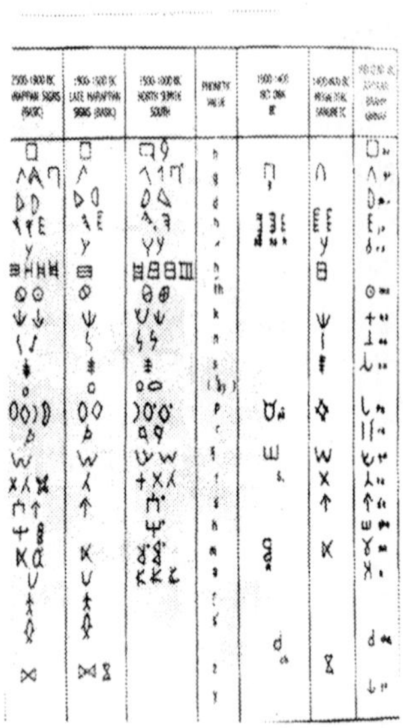

Fig. 41 : Necklace, C. 2600-2000 B.C. Lothal Gold, Loan from Lothal Museum A.S.I. National Museum, New Delhi Collection.

SEALS AND SCRIPT

The majority of the mysterious seals, carved mostly on square pieces of steatite, bear engravings of animals with a short inscription (Fig. 43). Since the mystery of the script is still on the

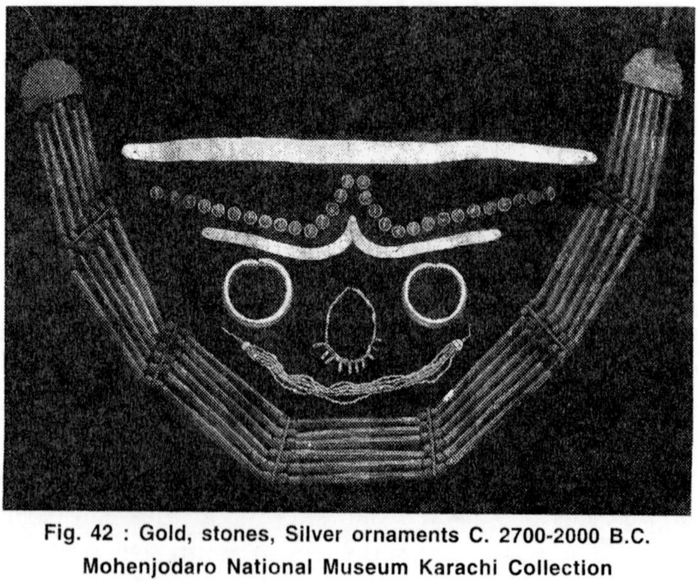

Fig. 42 : Gold, stones, Silver ornaments C. 2700-2000 B.C. Mohenjodaro National Museum Karachi Collection

Fig. 43 : Seals from Mohenjodaro Pakistan Collection

way to decipherment we do not know what the engravings mean. The animals generally include the elephant, the bull and the unicorn. Other seals depict the mother goddess and some ritualistic scenes, which give the impression that the seals, although used as stamps of authority in trade, represented religious symbols used during the rituals. The Indus inscriptions yet to be deciphered were using two languages i.e. Brahui and Sanskrit and their script was perhaps proto-Brahmi.

The Harappan Script now available from about 5515 inscriptions from various excavated remains is on the way to decipherment. No bilingual inscriptions has been found so far except two eastern island type brick inscriptions of the Mature Harappan period from western U. P. and the late Harappan biscriptal inscription from Bet Dwarika (Fig. 44). Parpola's claim of the Indus script being proto Dravidian in Brahui language may be correct. The claim by some other scholars (S. R. Rao) that the script is proto Brahmi and in Sanskrit language may also be correct. B. B. Lal has observed that the writing direction of the Harappan script was mostly from right to left. S. P. Gupta and Raja Ram say that the writing system was mostly from left to right. A few other scholars have suggested that the writing

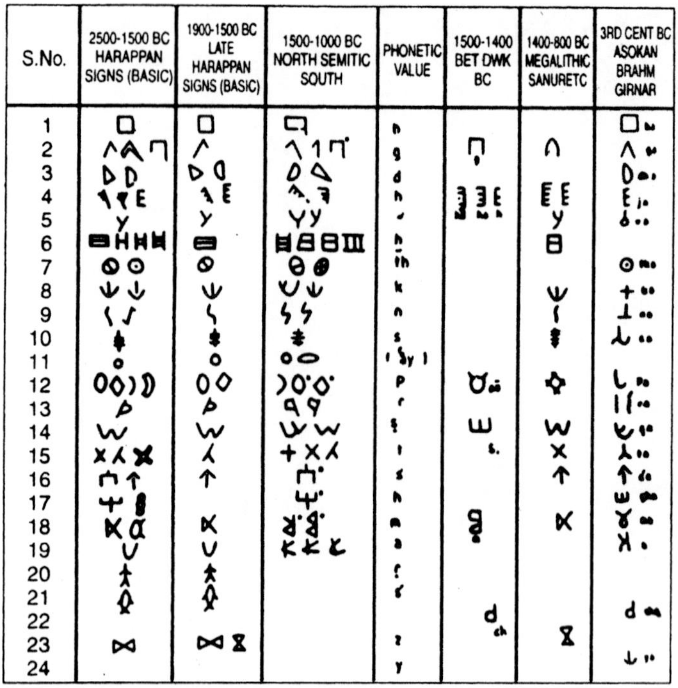

Fig. 44 : Comparative study of Bet Dwarika inscriptions with other scripts after S.R. Rao, 2001.

direction of the Harappan script was bostrophedon (both sides). During the Mature Harappan period circa 2700-2000 B. C. the direction of the Harappan writing system was mostly from right to left and later on around 2000 -1500 B.C. (end of late Harappans) they started their writing system from left to right. We get the Harappan script in an inscription found at Bet Dwarika. The discovery of a long written inscription and a bilingual inscription could only solve the problem of decipherment of the Harappan script. The recent discovery of an inscribed double-headed terracotta figurine from Kalibangan gives some impression of a Harappan script bearing a Proto-Brahmi script. The present author (D.P. Sharma) and other scholars read this inscription as *SIVAM* शिवम् (Fig. 45)

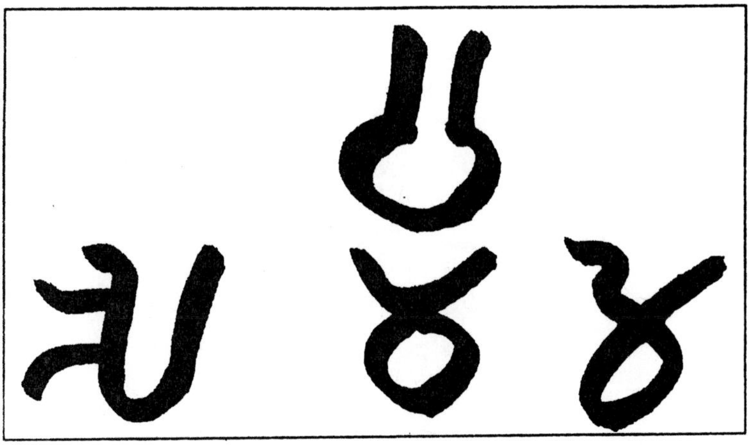

Fig. 45 : Double headed human figure, inscribed portion, Kalibangan C. 2000-1900 B.C.

POTTERY

The potteries, excavated at Harappa, Nal, Nausharo, Kalibangan, Dhalewan, Sothi, Lothal, Dholavira, Rakhigarhi, Mohenjo-daro and at other centres of the Civilization, was made on a potter's wheel and was fired or baked at a high temperature (Fig. 46). There seems to have been pottery jars in particular of a wide range of standard shapes and forms used for a variety of purposes. Distinct among the

Fig. 46 : Potter of Harappa making replica of storage jar. Photograph after Kenoyer; 1998, p. 151.

pottery of this period are large storage jars, tall perforated cylindrical vessels and dishes-on stands. Many of these are decorated with designs in black, depicting pipal and other leaves, animals, stories, fish, fish-scales and intersecting circles. A few potsherds even have graffiti marks bearing symbols and letters. The early Harappan Ceramics from Rakhigarhi, Kalibangan, Dhalewan, Dholavira, Harappa, Nal, Kunal, Dholavira shows the origin of Harappan Pottery. The perforated red ware Jar is a typical characteristic of the Harappan civilization (Fig. 47).

Fig. 47 : Perforated Jar, red ware, used in some rituals, C. 2700 B.C. Harappa National Museum New Delhi Collection.

RELIGION AND RITUALS

Fire worship was a typical characteristic of the Mature Harappans and there are evidences from Lothal, Kalibangan, Rakhigarhi and Banawali (Fig. 48). The fire worship shows the influence of Atharvavedic Aryans. The

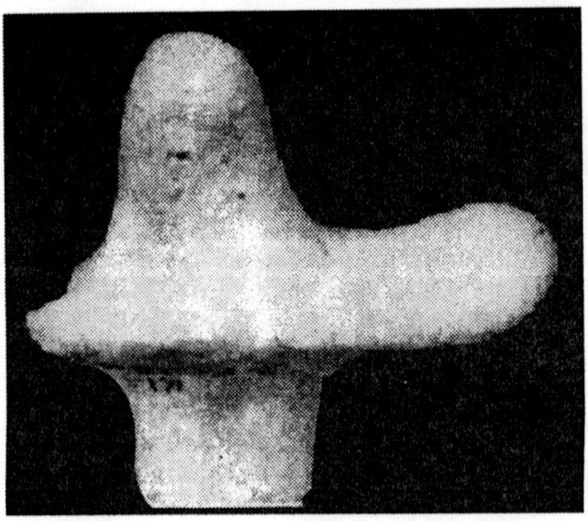

Fig. 48 : Terracotta *Sivalinga* Mature Harappan period (2600-2000 B.C.) Kalibangan. Loan from A.S.I. Acc. No. 12965, Neg No. 229-2000 (N.M.) National Museum, New Delhi Collection.

cult of Siva and Sakti (mother goddess) was an important religion of the Mature Harappans. The worship of a horned deity called Pasupati, Earth Goddesses, the Linga and Yoni, other sacrifices, the pipal tree, Bangle worship, snake worship and yoga were the other facets of Harappan religion and rituals. Some religious practices and the influence of the Early Harappans (Rigvedic and Yajurvedic) also continued during the Mature Harappan (Fig. 49).

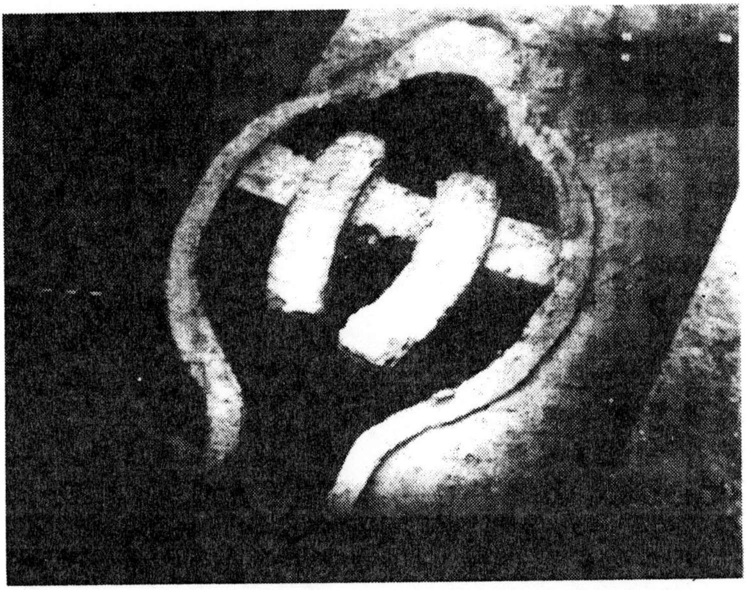

Fig. 49 : Yoni shaped potter kiln, shows influence of Vedic Aryan, C. 2800-2600 B.C. Rakhigarhi excavated by Amrendranath Neg No. 12-2000 (N.M.)

MEDICINE AND SURGERY

The Harappan burials at Kalibangan and Lothal bear evidences of trephination i.e. brain surgery. A similar evidence of trephination was reported from Burzahom, which is an early Neolithic site in Kashmir contemporary with the early Mature Harappans.

TOOLS AND WEAPONS

The National Museum, New Delhi has a number of copper tools from Harappan sites. These include flat axes, chisels, knives, fish hooks and a small saw (Fig. 50). Although the cities of the Harappan Civilization generally had protective walls and bastions around them, it is believed that they did not develop any sophisticated weaponry. Only simple spearheads and arrowheads have been found. These people were basically peace-loving traders and agriculturists. Long chert stone blades reported from Harappan sites is a peculiarity of the Mature Harappans.

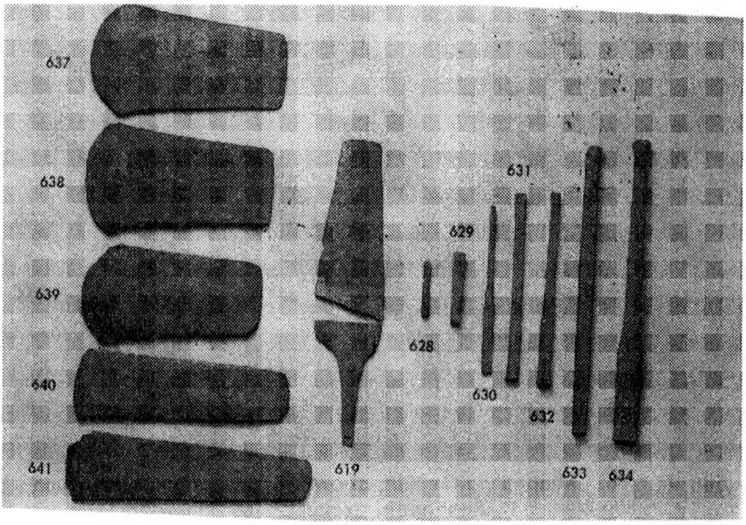

Fig. 50 : Copper flat axes, spear-head and chisels, C. 2700 B.C. Mohenjodaro, National Museum, Karachi Collection after Kondo 2001

BURIAL

The dead were usually buried in extended position with head towards the north. The offerings in graves generally included earthen pots and pans. The personal ornaments like bangles, necklaces, anklets, finger-rings, ear rings, etc., were sometimes found on the skeletons. At

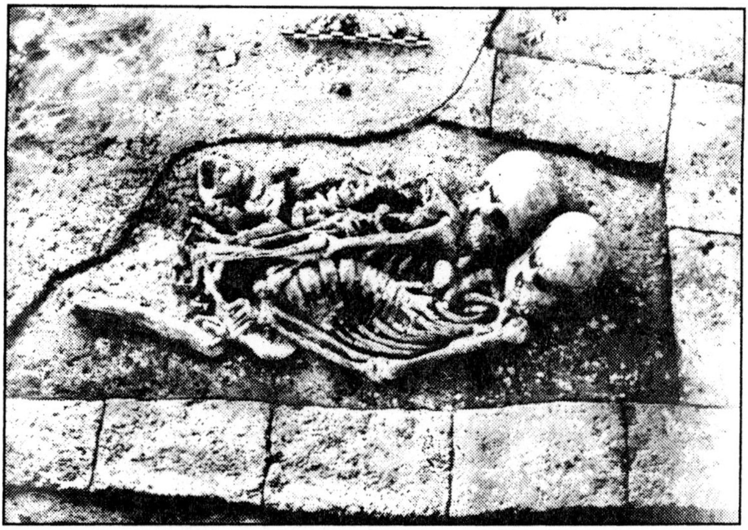

Fig. 51 : Skeleton of two individuals (Male and Female) C. 2600-2000 B.C. Lothal, A.S.I. Lothal Site Museum. Neg No. 1113-1996 (N.M.)

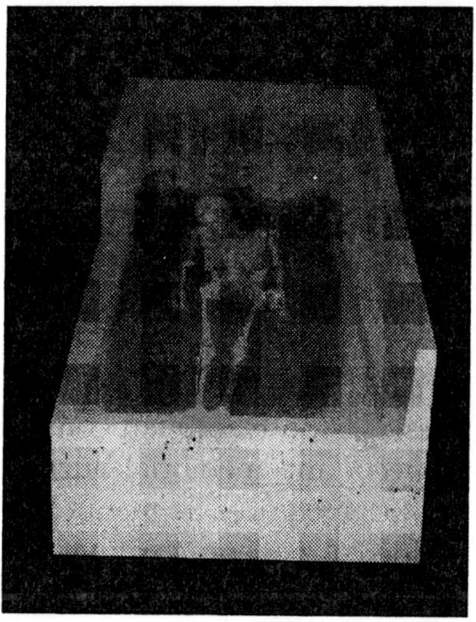

Fig. 52 : Extended Burial head toward north with offerings in graves (Harappan pots) C. 2600-2000 B.C., Rakhigarhi. Photograph by J.C. Arora.

Lothal, some burials have yielded skeletons of two individuals together (Fig. 51). At Kalibangan, some large pots, with or without human bones, were buried in pits, possibly as memorials. The Harappans were also cremating their dead bodies. A complete human burial of the Mature Harappan from Rakhigarhi is on display in the Harappan gallery of the National Museum, New Delhi (Fig. 52).

The mature Harappan burials were of three types: (1) extended (2) rectangular pot burial with bones and (3) circular or oval pot burial mostly without bones.

At Kalibangan there are evidences of the modes of disposal of the dead i.e.perhaps *'Nadi Pravah'* (flowing in the river) and cremation. The burials were reported from Mature Harappan sites like Surkotada and ortho-state type cairn circle, and a row of barrow burial of *Rath-chiti* burials at Dholavira suggests similarities with the megalithic and Buddhist tradition of later period. This evidence suggests the existence of memorial burial and perhaps cremation. The variation in the Harappan burial types and *Nadi Pravah* is also indicative of different groups. S. R. Rao, D.P. Sharma and J. P. Joshi are of the opinion that *"Most of the Aryans seem to have changed from inhumation burial to cremation in the Rigvedic period is clear from the Rigvedic verses VII 39. Rigvedic literature was composed during second millennium B. C. and the actual period of Rigvedic event could be dated between fourth and early third millennium B.C."*

The discovery of the coffin type burials from Harappa and the *Bhumigraha* type from Kalibangan supports the various types of disposal of the dead, which have been described in detail in the *Atharvaveda* and *Rigveda Samhitas*. J. P. Joshi has given reference of the Vedic literature as follows. There are different types of the trunks of trees; *Bhumigrah; Agnidagdha; Parokta,* (Cast aside); *Uddhitah* (deposited in trees and caves). In the Harappan context there are evidences of *Mukhagani* and memorial burials. These tally well with the Vedic references as mentioned above. We need more archaeological evidence to prove that the Harappans were Rigvedic Aryans which is lacking. However, we can say that the early Harappans were contemporary of Rigvedic people and their influence and legacy continued during the Mature Harappan period.

INDUSTRY

Fig. 53 : Necklace, beads in preparing stage, weight and pot for keeping water C. 2700 B.C. Harappa Site Museum Harappa Collection.

Industrial base is an important feature of any urban civilization. The making of beads with carnelian and other stones was an important feature of the Mature Harappans of Gujarat and other states (Fig. 53). The Copper/Bronze industry was an important industry of the Mature Harappans. The Harappan Copper/Bronze industry was flourishing at Mohenjo-daro, Harappa, Chanhudaro, Lothal, Kuntasi and Dholavira. Copper smelting furnaces, Susa type copper ingots and melted copper and crucibles were discovered from Mature Harappan sites. The Harappans knew copper-casting and the hammering technique. The two dancing girls from Mohenjo-daro and the animals from Daimabad, all made of copper, show the high perfection of indigenous sculpturing during Harappan times. The separate rows of copper smith quarters found at Lothal and Harappa confirm the existence of the copper-casting technique at the Harappan sites. Copper implements have been reported from all the Mature Harappan sites. Copper, gold and silver utencil shapes are copies of Harappan ceramics (Fig. 54).

The Shell industry has been reported from Lothal, Nageshwar, Allahdino, Dholavira, Mohenjodaro and other Harappan sites. Nageshwar was a shell industry

Fig. 54 : Copper Cooking Handi (612) C. 2700 B.C. Harappa. Tumbler made of green felds par stone C. 2700 B.C. Mohenjodaro. Both National Museum, Karachi Collection.

centre of the Mature Harappan period. Shell fragments of ladles, bangles and inlay pieces along with fragments of chank shell were found in the excavations at Nageshwar which confirms the flourishing of shell industry of the Mature Harappans on the north western coast of South Asia. The Mature Harappans grew cotton. The cotton clothes were noticed on the figurines and stone sculptures of the Harappan period. A piece of cotton cloth was found at Mohenjo-daro, which is now in the collection of Pakistan. Cloth impressions are found on the terracotta sealings from Lothal, Kalibangan and other sites. The discovery of a number of spindle whorls suggests that the Mature Harappans were making yarn.

Chanhudaro was a seal-making centre. A large number of unfinished seals in various stages have been found along with engravings and the metallic equipment needed for the seal industry. For the industrial base the Harappans needed raw material and markets for their finished products. There is ample evidence of internal and external long distance trade during the Mature Harappan period.

TRANSPORT

For the Harappans trade and movement of people in transport was very important. Animals like camels, elephants, horses and asses were used for transport of men and materials. A bronze model of two-wheeled carts at Harappa, Chanhudaro, Mohenjo-daro and Daimabad has confirmed that the Harappans were using these for land transport. The cart models and solid wheels made of terracotta discovered from the Harappan sites suggest that bullock carts were the most popular mode of transport (Fig. 55).

Fig. 55 : Model of bullock cart (Wooden part restored) C. 2700 B.C. Mohenjodaro Terracotta, National Museum, Karachi Collection.

Flat-bottomed boats were used for transport in rivers and lakes. The models of boats from Lothal and the depiction of a boat on a seal from Mohenjo-daro suggests the existence of sea transport. The Harappans were using these boats in their sea journeys to West Asia (Fig. 56).

Fig. 56 : Boat and its modern model. C. 2500 B.C., Lothal, Terracotta, Neg No. 3-2000. National Museum, New Delhi Collection.

AGRICULTURE

The discovery of a Harappan ploughed field from Kalibangan indicates the pattern of ploughing (Fig.57). The terracotta models of a plough from Banawali and Kalibangan suggests the shape of the plough-share, which is not much different from the present ones (Fig. 58). The Harappans' main food was wheat, barley, rice, ragi and

Fig. 57 : Plough field. Early Harappan (C-3000-2700 B.C.) Kalibangan, District Ganganagar (Now Hanumangarh) Photograph after B.B. Lal; 1997

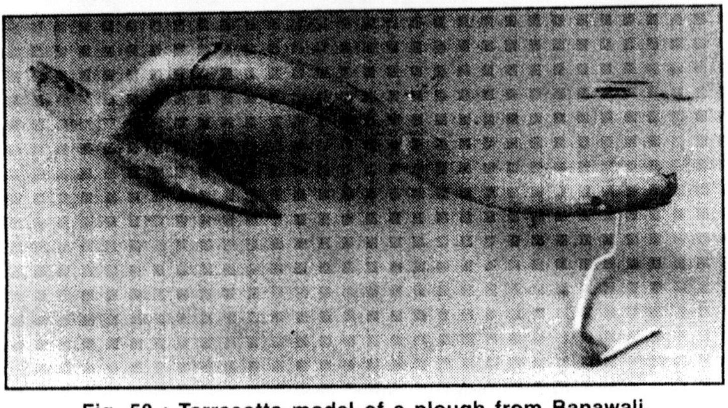

Fig. 58 : Terracotta model of a plough from Banawali, Mature Harappan period C. 2600-2000 B.C.

jowar. The evidence of granaries from Mohenjo-daro, Harappa and Lothal indicates surplus food production. The Harappans of Allahdino were masters in hydraulic engineering. The discovery of 18 reservoirs from Dholavira suggests that the Mature Harappans were excellent at water management. This also suggests the existence of reservoirs which were used for potable water and bunds for irrigation purposes. A Harappan period canal in the Ghaggar-Hakra plain was exposed by Frankfort. They were expert cotton producers and Harappan cotton was exported to Iran and Mesopotamia. The Harappans also cultivated grapes. The West Asian millets like jowar and bajra were introduced at the Harappan sites from the Gulf region. Oil seeds, sesame and mustard have also been reported from Harappan sites. These oil items could be the cooking mediums of the Harappans and also for lighting lamps. Besides the above agricultural produces, the Mature Harappans supplemented their food with the meat of domesticated and wild animals e.g. cattle, buffaloes, sheep, goats, pigs and rodents. Bones of chicken have been found at Harappan sites. The Mature Harappans also practised animal husbandry and poultry farming. The discovery of a large number of terracotta bulls from Rakhigarhi and other Harappan sites also confirms the same. Stone mortar of the mature Harappan period was also discovered from Rakhigarhi (Fig. 59).

Fig. 59 : Cubical Harappan weights showing ratio of 4 : 8, C. 2600 B.C. Banawali, Loan from A.S.I. National Museum, New Delhi Collection.

TRADE

(A). INTERNAL TRADE

J. P. Joshi is of the opinion *"That the Mature Harappans internal trade could have been done through the guilds in an organised fashion on major items but the non-organised trade was done by nomads at individual levels. The items included natural produces, some metallic handicrafts and spices and some herbal medicines, etc."*

The Khetri area of Rajasthan supplied the copper-ore to the Mature Harappans. The Rajpipla and Khambat area in Gujarat supplied semiprecious stones to the Harappans. The Harappans of Punjab, Haryana, Baluchistan and western Uttar Pradesh supplied surplus wheat and barley. The Gujarat regions used to supply Bajra, jowar and cotton. Shells came from the coastal region of Gujarat and Sindh. Steatite seals were supplied from Chanhudaro. J. P. Joshi has observed, *"that the internal trade was conducted by guilds that had their own seals and tablets. The base towns were Mohenjo-daro yielding 1540 seals and Harappa 1100 seal and sealings which are made of steatite, terracotta, copper, silver and other material.* Mark Kenoyer suggested,*"As a totemic symbol the animal represented a specific clan or official. At least ten clans of communities are represented by these totemic animals"*. The present author (D.P. Sharma) is

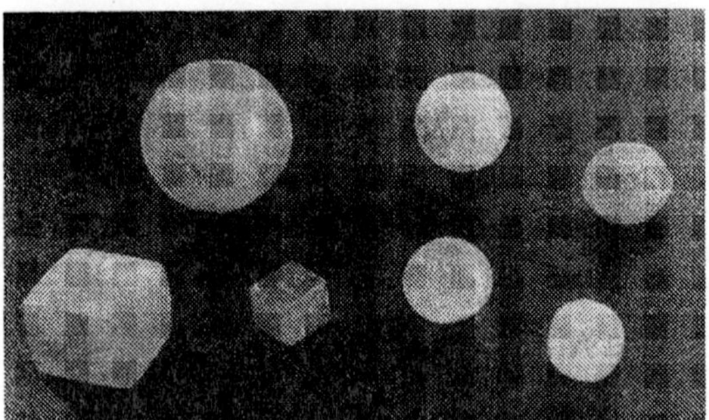

Fig. 60 : Cubical (Harappan) and round weights of various ratio 2:4:8 of west Asian type (Bahrain). C. 2600 B.C., Dholavira. Loan from A.S.I. National Museum, New Delhi Collection.

of the opinion that the above observation of Joshi and Kenoyer requires some more archaeological evidence, which is at present lacking. The standard system of Harappan weights and measures that was followed throughout confirms some authority over trade (Fig.60).

(B). EXTERNAL TRADE

During Circa 2700-1900 B.C. the Harappans were having trade contacts with Mesopotamia and other regions of West Asia. Bahrain played the vital role of a halfway house transmitting cultural cross currents from the east to the west. The discovery of a tidal dockyard at Lothal has confirmed the archaeological evidence of the maritime activities of the Mature Harappans. The discovery of the Bahrain type seals at Lothal and the Mesopotamian type cylindrical seals from Kalibangan, Mohenjo-daro and Rakhigarhi shows trade contacts between the Mature Harappan and West Asian region. The other Harappan port towns are Kuntasi, Padri, Dholavira and Prabhas patan. The Harappan traders had colonies at Urs in Mesopotamia. On the basis of the Mesopotamian inscription their trade in the eastern region was with Dilmun, Makran (Magan) and Meluhha. The Persian Gulf area is identified as Dilmun, Magan as Makran coast and Meluhha as Katch or Mohenjo-daro or Ganeshwar. On the basis of an Akkadian inscription we can say that boats from Meluhha or Harappan region were bringing carnelian, ivory, shell, timber, textile and copper. Harappan archaeologists have identified Magan with Oman (Fig. 61).

The Harappan objects like seals, carnelian beads, figurines, shells and ivory dice have been reported from Tell Asmar, Kish, Lagash, Umma, Nippur, Tepa Gawra, Jokha, Tell Agrab and Ashur which objects have the confirmed Harappans's trade links with Mesopotamia. The Harappan cubical stone weights and dozens of Persian Gulf

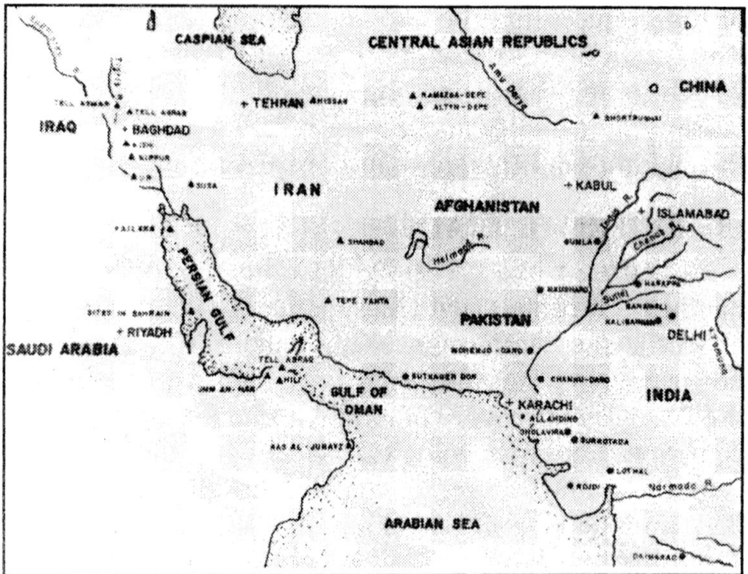

Some Sites With Harappan Artefacts (Outside the Homeland) ▲

Fig. 61 : Harappan artifacts discovered from outside of Harappan region C. 2500-2000 B.C. showing Harappan trade contacts, Neg No. 427-2000 (N.M.) Photograph after Possehl 2000.

type seals reported at Ras-al-Qala in Bahrain show some sort of partnership between the Mature Harappans and Persian Gulf merchants. The Mehi (Harappan) type copper mirror reported from Barbar (West Asia) also supports the trade links. At Hammad (Bahrain) archaeologists have reported about the Harappan seals with the engravings of the Harappan charging bull, peacock and five Harappan graffities, which show the contacts between the Harappan region and Bahrain.

At Rosal Junyaj in Oman the discovery of a Harappan seal and pottery with four graffities and the pottery from Hili with a painted peacock and pipal tree shows the Harappan influence. At Shortugai located near Badakshan in the Oxus region in Afghanistan the mines of lapis-lazuli might have attracted the Harappan merchants who had exploited these mines for their lapis beads industry. The Harappan traders were having settlements at Altyn Depe and Namazga tepe in Turkmania where Harappan seals and sealings have been reported. The terracotta model of an Egyptian mummy, a West Asian human head and Gorilla from Lothal, West Asian hairpins from Harappan sites and reserved slip wares of west Asian origin from Surkotada, Lothal, Dholavira and Mohenjo-daro also support the existence of trade relations between the Harappans and West Asia (Fig. 62).

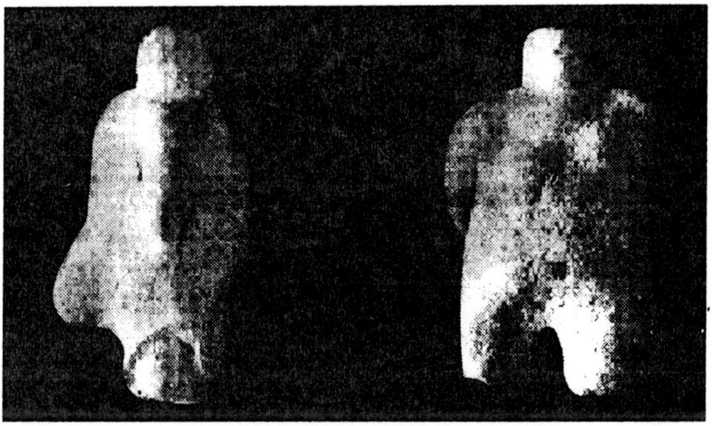

Fig. 62 : Terracotta model of African Gorilla, C. 2500 B.C. Lothal Neg. No. 7-2000 (N.M.) National Museum, New Delhi Collection

The above evidence suggests the Harappan maritime trade with Mesopotamia, Egypt and the Persian Gulf during circa 2700-1800 B. C. We may conclude that the earliest record (inscription) for direct trade contacts between the Mature Harappan (Meluhha) and Mesopotamia (West Asia) hails from the region of Sargon (circa 2334-2279 B. C.). According to the archaeological evidence this trade flourished throughout the Akkadian and Ur III periods and continued down into I sin Larsa Period (circa 2017-1763 B.C.). The other Mesopotamian records mention Magan

(Oman), which confirms long distance trade down the Persian Gulf into the Harappan region. The cone inscription of Nammu King of Ur (circa 2112-2095 B. C.) Ur III period mentions about the ship of Magan (Oman).

In addition to the textual evidence a number of Harappan seals were found in the sites of Mesopotamia, which also confirm the Harappan trade contacts with West Asia. These seals are circular and are made of steatite and have a single groove across the back. Vessels of soft stone (Chlorite) made in Iran and Afghanistan were traded up to the Indus region. Such vessels discovered from Mohenjo-daro, Dholavira and Lothal suggest trade links with West Asia.

LATE HARAPPAN

The Harappan urban phase ended around c 2000-1900 B. C. The Harappan Civilization ended due to massive flooding, climatic changes and increase of aridity, tectonic movements and decline of trade with West Asia. According to B.B. Lal, S. Ratnagar, Nayanjot Lahiri and D.P. Sharma the Aryan invasion theory of massacre at Harappan sites does not hold any ground. Sareen Ratnagar and S. Asthana has suggested that the collapse of the distant trade mechanism and population explosion and over-use of land resources set a devolutionary process that brought about the decline of the Harappan Civilization during the first quarter of second millennium B.C. (Fig. 63).

The late Harappan Culture (circa 1900-1500 B.C.) shows a stage of de-urbanization after the mature phase of the Harappans. The late Harappan village Chalcolithic Culture is characterized by the absence of monumental architecture, big settlements, citadel and lower town i.e. two divisions of town planning, inscriptions devoid of Harappan animals, long chert blades. However, the pottery shapes of the Mature Harappans continued. It appears that

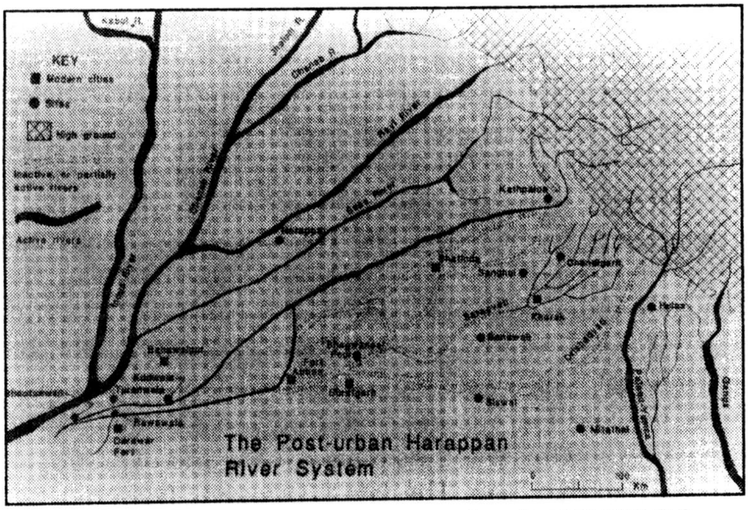

Fig. 63 : Post Harappan–late Harappan sites C. 1900-1500 B.C. Neg. No. 2/42, 2000 Photograph after Possehl, 2000.

during the late Harappan period surplus food production, distance trade with West Asia and the strong hold of central authority did not exist. Recent excavations at Mandi and Quetta where large jewellery hoards come to light suggests that the late Harappans were familiar with the Mature Harappan type gold and silver ornaments which shows the mature Harappan legacy (Fig. 64).

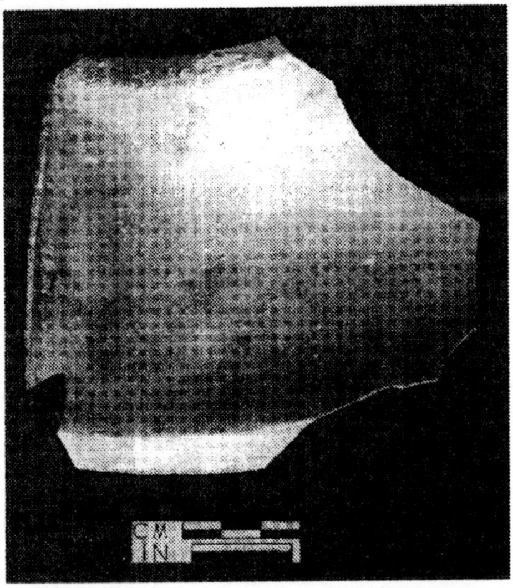

Fig. 64 : Part of utencil (dish), Silver, Mandi, C. 2000-1900 B.C. Mature Late Harappan Transition stage. Loan from A.S.I. National Museum, New Delhi Collection.

During the late Harappan period the Harappan urban process could not survive. According to J. P. Joshi the hydrological changes adversely affecting the availability of water in the lower and middle courses of the perennial river system like the Ghaggar (Hakra) or Saraswati made the Harappans to leave their settlements and break their urban fabric forever. The late Harappans preferred the alluvial fertile regions of eastern Punjab, Haryana and upper Ganga-Yamuna doab of western U.P. because this area still retained water in the rivers besides easy availability of timber and mineral, which were the essential needs of these people. Now the late Harappans preferred the nearby area of tributaries and this was the situation in the area of the upper Ganga-Yamuna doab. The late Harappans favoured the tributaries of the Yamuna. There are around 200 Late Harappan sites situated on the bank of Krishni, Kali and Hindon rivers, which are tributaries of the Yamuna. During circa 1600-1000 B.C. river Saraswati joined the Yamuna somewhere between Ambala and Hisar.

The late Harappan sites are smaller in size, located on a higher elevation at a distance of 5 to 12 km and had close contacts and communication with each other. These have an agricultural base. In Rajasthan and the Upper Ganga-Yamuna doab region the late Harappans were associated with ochre coloured ware and copper hoard culture. Some mature Harappan shapes are present in O.C.P. The O.C.P. existed in India from circa 2800- 1000 B. C. and they were having contacts with the early, mature and late Harappans. We can associate O.C.P. people with the village Chalcolithic Culture of the Atharvavedic period and they were different from the Harappans. The copper hoard culture was also contemporary with the Mature Harappan and late Harappan culture and they were different from the Harappans. Archaeologists have certain reservations about the labeling of O.C.P. as late Harappan. The copper hoard objects like the Anthropomorphic figures and harpoons found in the Harappan deposits of Lothal, Madarpur and Mitathal suggest that the copper hoard people of western group were contemporary with the Mature Harappan. O.C.P. and Anthropomorphic figures of copper hoard culture have been reported from Saipai and Madarpur. The typical Harappan shapes like the perforated pot were found in the O.C.P. ceramics of Madarpur which infact confirms some relation between the two cultures . We can conclude that the copper hoard people, the O.C.P. people and Mature Harappan were contemporary.

J. P. Joshi has observed, that the O.C.P. culture of upper doab represented by Ambakheri was derived from Mitathal B where copper hoard and harpoon were also found and is the second in the central doab of western Uttar Pradesh and Haryana represented by Atranjikhera, Jakhera and Saipai where a copper Anthropomorphic figure was found. We need some more sites where we get the O.C.P. and copper hoard together. We can thus conclude that the O.C.P. and copper hoards began during the Early and Mature Harappan periods and continued contemporary to the late Harappan time. We associate the copper hoard and O.C.P. with the Atharvavedic Aryans.

The excavations at Hulas, Dadheri, Katpalon, Harappa, Nagar, Bhagwanpura, Siswal, Mitathal, Mirzapur, Balu, Bet Dwarika, Banawali, Alamgirpur, Ambakheri, Mandi, Mandavali and Bhorgarh have given more details of the late Harappan Culture of India.

At Mandi, Dadheri, Sanghol, Mandavali and Bhorgarh the late Harappan culture was followed by the Painted grey ware culture. At Bhagwanpura there is an overlap of Late Harappan and painted grey ware cultures. The discovery of a 13-room mud house at Bhagwanpura shows the influence and legacy of the Mature Harappan culture. A similar situation we notice at Bhorgarh and Mandavali in Delhi.

Mitathal II B and Daulatpur I deposit too belongs to the late Harappan culture. The deposits of PdII of Banawali are Bara culture, which is contemporary of the late Harappan. The deposit of phase C. of Bara belongs to the late Harappan and Bara culture.

Alamgirpur period I is also late Harappan and the shapes in the ceramics of this phase are dishes-on-stand, goblets with pointed base, beakers, shallow basins and goblets with a concave neck and elongated base. The ceramic is red slipped ware decorated with black designs. The designs include bands, intersecting circles, plants and peacocks. The pottery also has black and hatched designs. There are evidences of kiln-burnt bricks and Harappan graffitis without animals. The beads of semi-precious stones, cakes, inscribed dishes-on-stand and some potteries have textile impressions. The archaeological material of Alamgirpur gives an impression of a Mature Harappan site. However, there is no evidence of Mature Harappan seals, chert blades and the systematic two divisions of Mature Harappan town planning. J. P. Joshi has rightly remarked that the late Harappan sites were succeeded by the painted Grey ware culture.

Hulas in western U.P. excavated by K.N. Dikshit is also a late Harappan site. The rectangular, circular and mud brick houses belong to the late Harappan phase. The ceramic is sturdy red ware and the motif is non mature Harappan. A unique find is a seal without a knob having three grafitties. There are evidences of cultivated rice, grams, ragi and barley. The excavations at Mahorana have revealed the presence of Bara ware, which overlapped, from the early Harappan to the late Harappan period. Bara is another ceramic and we can correlate this with the early Aryans. The inscribed red ware of the Early Harappan period of Kalibangan also continued during the late Harappan period in Punjab and Haryana. Cemetery H. Red ware of the late Harappan period of Harappa is present in Haryana, Punjab and Bahawalpur areas. The C^{14} date of the late Harappan period of Sanghol goes back to circa 1785-1500 B. C. and another date from Bhagwanpura to circa 1700 B.C. Thus we can date the late Harappan period from circa 2000 to 1500 B.C.

HARAPPAN LEGACY

The Harappan culture ended around circa 1600-1500 B.C. but its impact has been tremendous on the later Chalcolithic Iron age cultures. There is Harappan influence on the post Harappan Chalcolithic Cultures of Malva at Kaitha, Dangwada, Chichli and Northern Deccan. The long chert blades, thin disc beads of steatite, copper axes, painted pots, beads and burials showing late Harappan influence continued till 1000 B.C.

According to J. P. Joshi, "systematic town planning, the fortification of citadel, granaries, surplus production, weight and measures, compass, scale, plumb bob, pipal motif, the burial system, Swastika, seals, etc., are the gifts of the Harappans to the later cultures of South Asia. The maritime trade, bullock cart, wheat, Siva worship, yoga, sakti or mother goddess worship, chess and dance are the Harappan legacy." Prof B.B. Lal recently has observed in his new publication "Saraswati flows on" that Harappan traditions are still continuing.

We can say that our Harappan ancestors were neither aggressors nor conquerors. They were peace-loving traders. Their economy was mainly based on agriculture and trade.

THE DECLINE

The Harappan Civilization declined slowly and gradually when sites like Mohenjo-daro were repeatedly threatened by heavy floods in the river Indus. Kalibangan in Rajasthan, Banawali and Rakhigarhi in Haryana were situated on the banks of the river Saraswati and its drying up resulted in these settlements losing their very existence. Lothal and Dholavira in Gujarat suffered heavy losses in trade with Mesopotamia, and at Surkotada, Harappa, Rakhigarhi, Banawali, etc., man interfered with environment by cutting trees for fuel and grazing lands indiscriminately.

M.R. Sahni has confirmed the occurrence of earthquakes at Harappan sites. According to him a collision of earth plates resulted in the uplifting of the land and consequently the Indus river was damned leading to the submergence of large Mature Harappan sites. Dilip Chakraborti, Nayanjot Lahiri and Madhuri Sharma are of the opinion that all the reasons cited above caused the decline of the mature Harappan urban system.

HARAPPAN ARCHAEOLOGY : AN UPDATE

Some Harappan Archaeologists named Harappan Civilization as Saraswati Civilization and they prefer its name as Indus-Saraswati Civilization. The horse was known to the Harappans. Bisht and Bhagwan Singh are now of the opinion that the Harappans and Vedic people were the same. However, the present author (D.P. Sharma) is of the view that the early Harappan Village Chalcolithic Culture (circa 3500=2700 B.C.) and early Rigvedic and Yajurvedic were the same. The Early Harappan culture was village Chalcolithic culture and we can correlate the same with the Rigvedic, Yajurvedic culture. The Chalcolithic cultures of early Harappan are as follows:

(1) Togau phase C. 4300-3800 B.C.
(2) Kechi Beg Phase C. 3800-3200 B.C.
(3) Hakra Ware phase C. 3800-3200 B.C.
(4) Ravi Ware phase C. 3500-3300 B. C.

Mehrgarh III, Mundigak I-II-III, Rana Gundai III A and Sheri Khan Tarakai represent the Togau phase I (Fig. 65). The important Kechi Beg phase sites are Anjra, Sheri Khan- Tarakai, etc. The Hakra ware phase sites are Amri IA, Jalilpur and the lowest deposit of Harappa. According to Kenoyer and Kondo, the Poly Chrome Ravi Pottery from the lowest level was made before the advent of the early Harappans around circa 3500-3200 B. C. Ravi Ware is a

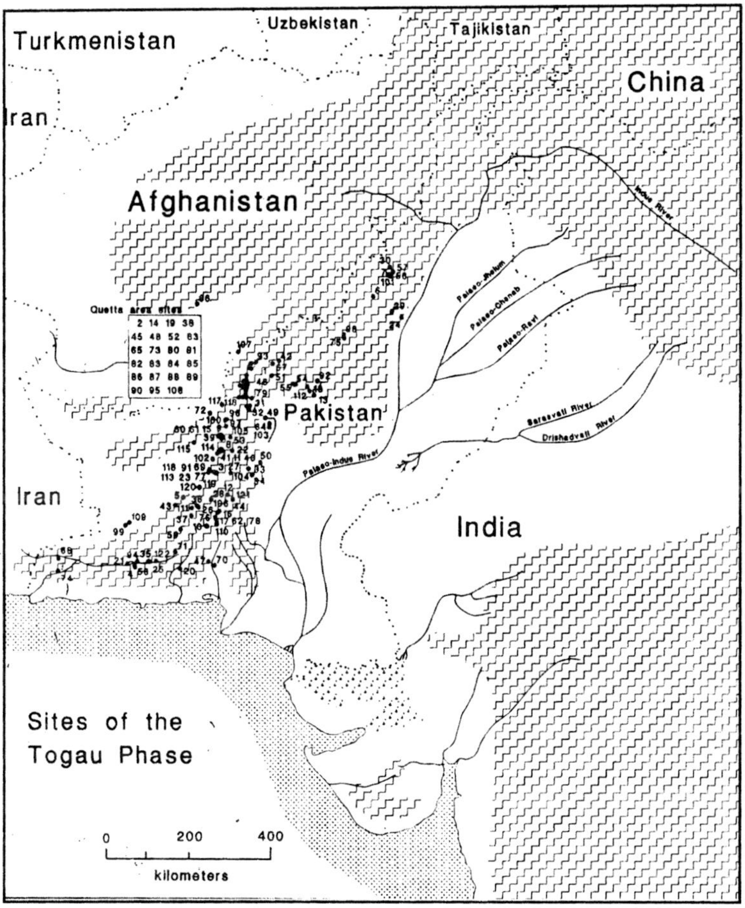

Fig. 65 : Sites of the Togau Phase.

hand-made ceramic and the designs are painted in shades of white, red and black. The motifs are intersecting circles, four petals and a waterfowl.

The Early Harappan (c.3500-2700 B.C.) was a developed village Chalcolithic culture and this preludes the Mature Harappan Civilization. A few important Early Harappan excavated sites are Amri (late phase), Nal, Anjira IV, Harappa early deposit, Nundara, Nagwada, Dholavira, Dhalewan early deposit, Padri, Somnath, Banawali Pd I A & B, Kotdiji, Nindawari, Kalibangan period I, Killi Gul Mohammad, Mehrgarh VII, Sothi, Siswal, Kunal Rehmandehri, etc.

Possehl (2000) has listed 2600 sites of Pre-Harappan, Mature Harappan, Late Harappan and other Harappan associated contemporary sites of O.C.P. / Copper hoard, etc. During the last few years 58 more Harappan sites have been discovered. Now we can say that so far around 2658 Harappan and its associated sites have been reported from the north western part of south Asia.

Horse bones, brick altars of rituals and copper hoard weapons have been discovered from the mature Harappan sites which show contacts between the early Atharvavedic Aryan and Harappan people.

Suggested Reading

Dhavalikar M. K.	1995	*Cultural Imperialism, Indus Civilization, Western India.* New Delhi.
Gupta S. P.	1997	*The Indus-Sarasvati Civilization.* New Delhi: Pratibha. Prakshan.
Joshi J. P. & R.S. Bisht	1994	*India and Indus Civilization* Delhi. National Museum, New Delhi

Joshi Jagatpati	2001	*Harappan Civilization as seen at the Close of the Twentieth Century* paper in M&E XXV(1). Poona
Kenoyer J. M.	1998	*Ancient Cities of the Indus Valley Civilization*. Karachi: Oxford University Press and the American Institute of Pakistan Studies.
Lal B. B.	1997	*The Earliest Civilization of South Asia: Rise, Maturity and Decline*. New Delhi: Aryan Book International.
Lal B. B.	1998	*New Light on the Indus Civilization*, New Delhi.
Lal B. B.	2001	*Saraswati Flows on*, Aryan Book International, New Delhi
Lahiri Nayanjot	1992	*The Archaeology of Indian Trade Routes up to circa 200 B.C.* New Delhi.
Lahiri Nayanjot D. Chakrabarti	1998	*Copper and its Alloys in Ancient Period*. New Delhi.
Nigam M. L.	2000	*Early Indian Jewellery*. New Delhi.
Possehl G. L.	2000	*Indus Age the Beginning*, New Delhi.
Ratnagar Shereen	2000	*The End of the Great Harappan Tradition*, New Delhi.
Ratnagar Shereen	2001	*Understanding Harappa Civilization in the Greater Indus Valley*, Mumbai.
Rao S. R.	2000	*Lost City of Dwarika*, Delhi.

Sharma D. V.	2000	*Harappan Jewellery Hoard from Mandi* paper in *Puratattva No. 30* Delhi.
Sharma D. P.	1999	*Bharat aur Sindhu Sabhyata.* (Hindi) New Delhi.
Sharma D. P.	2000	*Indus Script on its Way to Decipherment.* New Delhi.
Sharma D. P.	2000	*Harappan Seals, Sealings and Copper Tablets.* New Delhi.
Sharma D. P.	2002	*Harappan Terracottas.* New Delhi.
Sharma D. P.	2002	*Harappan Art,* Vol. I New Delhi.
Sharma D. P.	2003	*Harappan Jewellery,* New Delhi
Sharma D. P.	2003	*Bharat Ka Puratattva* (Hindi) Delhi.
Satayawadi. S.	1994	*Proto-historic Potteries of Indus Valley,* Delhi.

QUESTIONNAIRE

1. Names of some Harappan sites have been jumbled up. Arrange them in order.

U M R P I A L G A R	
G I N A A L K N A B	
E O M H D O A J R N O	
P N R G U A R	
A P P R H A A	
T O L A L H	
D A H O V I R A L	

2. The houses were situated along the roads. Every house was furnished with several rooms, a kitchen, a well and a bathroom around a courtyard. The drainge system was perfect. The house drains emptied all the waste water into the street drains.

   Look at the photographs carefully and answer the following questions:(Fig. 66a,b,c)

(i) Were the houses built of bricks and stone? Yes/No

(ii) Were the floors built of decorated tiles also? Yes/No

(iii) Were the drains always open? Yes/No

Fig. 66a

Fig. 66b

Fig. 66c

3. Tick the correct answer: (Fig. 67)

(i) It was discovered at :

(a) Lothal ☐

(b) Harappa ☐

(c) Mohenjo-daro ☐

(d) Kalibangan ☐

(ii) It may have been a place of :

(a) playing water sports ☐

(b) religious bathing ☐

(c) storing water for irrigation ☐

(d) reservoir for drinking water ☐

(e) use as a dock-yard ☐

Fig. 67

4. What are these strange things? (Fig. 68)

   Try guessing and write down their names from the suggested list.

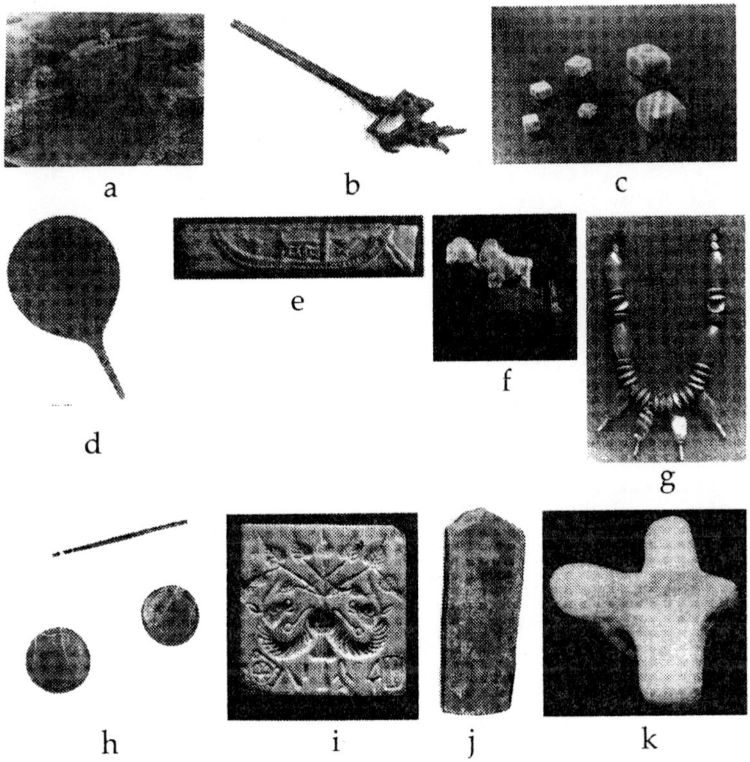

Suggested list:

- Animal-headed copper hairpin
- Gold and stone bead necklace
- Copper mirror
- Terracotta dice
- Terracotta sealing depicting boat.
- Terracotta toy animal with moveable head
- Scale
- Copper weighing balance and stone weights
- Copper fish-hook
- Steatite seal
- Bronze axe

5. This jar was used for storage.(Fig. 69)
Draw in what has been left out.

6. One of these pots was not used by the Harappan people (Fig. 70)

(a)

(b)

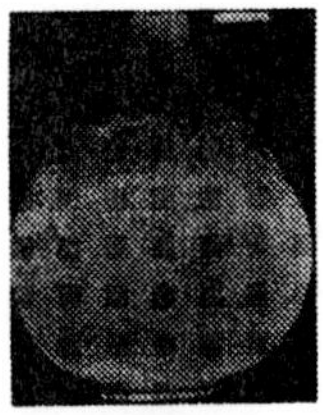

(c)

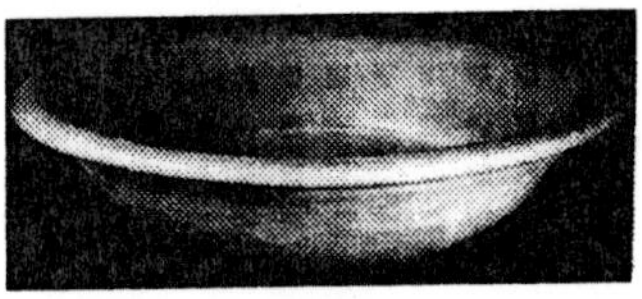

(d)

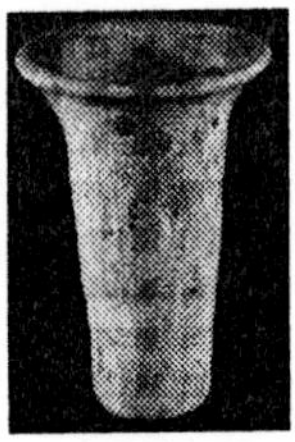

(e)

(f)

(g)

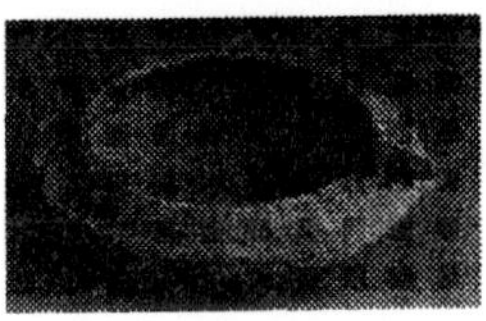

(h)

(i)

(i) Find that out..

(ii) From your observation in the gallery what do you learn about the

(a) Colours of the pottery..................................

(b) Designs on the pottery..................................

7. Tick mark the correct answer:(Fig. 71)

(i) This figure is generally called a

(a) fashionable lady ☐

(b) dancing girl ☐

(c) goddess ☐

(d) devotee ☐

(ii) This was discovered at

(a) Harappa ☐

(b) Lothal ☐

(c) Mohenjo-daro ☐

(d) Rangpur ☐

(iii) This is made of

(a) Iron ☐

(b) Bronze ☐

(c) Clay ☐

(d) Wood ☐

(iv) Name the technique by which it was made

....

8. Tick mark the correct answer:

(i) This female figure was (Fig. 72)

- (a) used for decoration ☐
- (b) buried with the dead ☐
- (c) used as a toy by the children ☐
- (d) worshipped as mother goddess ☐

(ii) This is made of

- (a) stone ☐
- (b) bronze ☐
- (c) clay ☐
- (d) wood ☐

(iii) This was made

- (a) from a mould
- (b) by hand modelling
- (c) using both the above techniques

(iv) Describe a few words about this figure of Banawali.

....

....

9. Crossword

(Fig. 73)

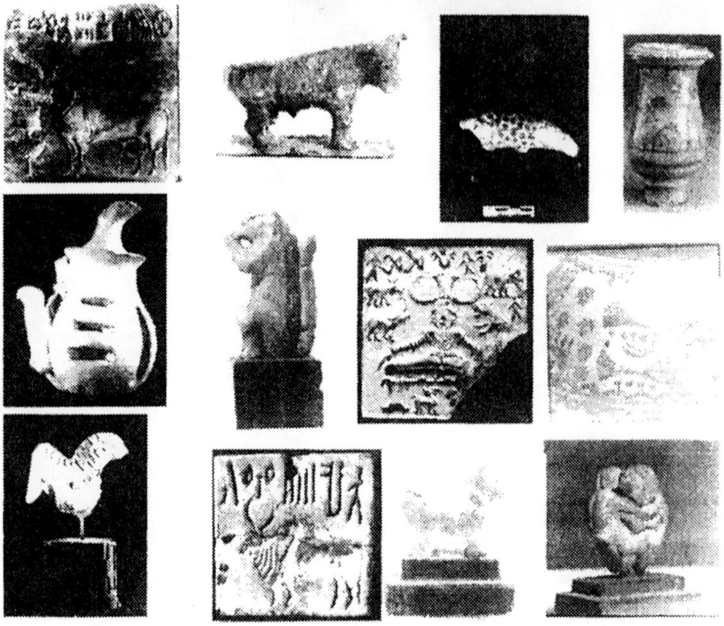

Here is a crossword puzzle based on the theme of the birds and animals known to the Harappan people with clues from various objects like seals, pots, toys, etc.

10. Carts with wheels were used for transportation. (Fig. 74)

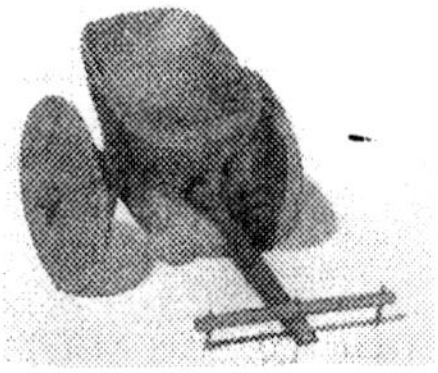

What was the animal yoked to it?

....

....

11. What do you infer from the discoveries of the dock-yard and the Persian Gulf seal at Lothal? (Fig. 75) (a-b)

....

....

a

b

12. This seal shows a seated figure surrounded by animal figures. What do you learn about the religion of the Harappan people from this seal and other objects illustrated on the previous pages? (Fig. 76)

Fig. 76

....

....

....

....

13. True or False

(i) The Harappan Civilization is one of the four oldest River Valley Civilizations of the world.

True/False

(ii) This civilization flourished between circa 2700 2000 B.C. in the northwestern regions of South Asia.

True/False

(iii) It is the indigenous civilization of the Indian sub-continent.

True/False

(iv) It had the oldest planned cities of the world.

True/False

(v) Some cities had huge granaries to store grain brought from the countryside.

True/False

(vi) Iron was used for implements and utensils .

True/False

(vii) There were no trade links between the Harappan sites, the Persian Gulf and the Mesopotamian sites.

True/False

(viii) The main roads were straight and wide, often cutting each other at right angles.

True/False

(ix) Pottery was made by hand alone.

True/False

(x) Wheat and barley were the staple food of the Harappan people. True/False

(xi) The elephant was one of the animals domesticated by the people of this civilization.

True/False

(xii) The script of this civilization has been satisfactorily deciphered. True/False

14. The dead were buried with the things which they used in their lifetime (Fig. 77).

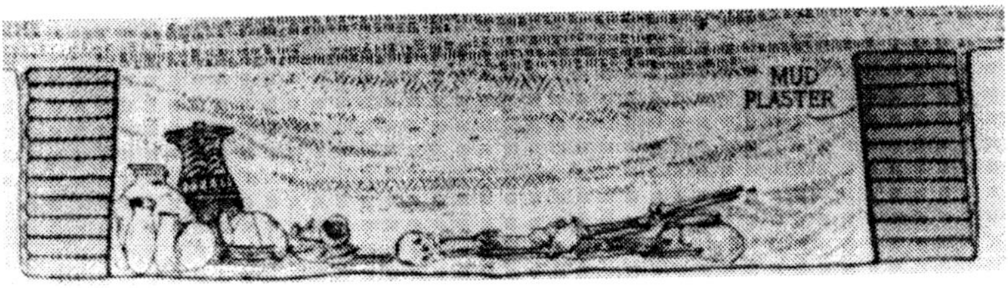

Fig. 77

(i) List some of the objects

....

....

....

(ii) Name the place where two bodies were found buried in a single grave.

....

15. From the objects depicted on the previous pages enumerate the various occupations of the people.

....

....

....

16. Here are some symbols and designs from the objects illustrated on the previous pages. (Fig. 78)

(a) What are these?

(b) Write down the names of the objects from which these have been taken.

a...............

b...............

a...............

b...............

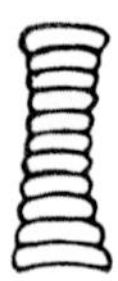

a...............

b...............

a...............

b...............

a...............

b...............

17. We cut this picture of a seal by mistake. Can you fit the pieces back together again and name what animal it has on it? (Fig. 79)

Fig. 79

18. What was the period of the mature Harappan Civilization?
19. Who did the first excavation on the Harappan site?
20. Who discovered the Harappan Civilization?
21. Name the largest mature Harappan site.

22. Please write a few words on the Harappan Civilization.

23. Were the mature Harappan and Rigvedic people the same?

24. Was the horse known to the mature Harappan?

25. Is the Harappan script deciphered? Write a few words on Harappan writing.

26. Write a few words on the religion and ritual of the mature Harappan.

27. Who discovered Mohenjo-daro?

28. How many Harappan and its associated sites have been explored and excavated? Name a few important sites.

29. What was the extension of the Harappan Civilization?

30 (A)Which is the largest mature Harappan site (write the correct answer)

(a) Ganwariwala	(h) Kalibangan	(o) Mehrgarh
(b) Harappa	(i) Padri	(p) Rojdi
(c) Mohenjo-daro	(j) Kuntasi	(q) Mandi
(d) Lothal	(k) Nausharo	(r) Hulas
(e) Dholavira	(l) Allahdino	(s) Banawali
(f) Dhalewan	(m) Daimabad	(t) Bet Dwarika
(g) Rakhigarhi	(n) Chanhudaro	(u) Gulf of Cambay

30(B). What was the time span of the mature Harappan Civilization (write correct answer?)

(a) circa 3500-2800 BC

(b) circa 2000-1500 BC

(c) circa 2700-2000 BC

(d) circa 3000-2000 BC

31. What was the nucleus region of the Harappan Civilization?

32. True and False:

    (a) The Harappan was an iron Age Civilization.

    (b) The Harappan had long distance trade with Mesopotamia.

    (c) The Harappan Civilization was indigenous in its growth.

    (d) The Harappan script has been fully deciphered.

    (e) Usually the Harappan towns were divided into two parts: the citadels and the lower town.

33. Rakhigarhi was an important craft centre during Harappan times (write correct answer).

34. What were the materials used for building houses of the mature Harappans?

35(A) The famous Great Bath is situated at which site?

(a) Mohenjo-daro	(e) Dholavira
(b) Harappa	(f) Shortaghai
(c) Banawali	(g) Kotdiji
(d) Lothal	(i) Mitathal

35(B) Fire worship was a typical characteristic of the mature Harappans. True or False?

36. Which animals are mostly depicted on the Harappan seal?

37. Two bronze dancing girls were found in Harappa. True or False?

38. What were the modes of transportation during the mature Harappan period?

39. What were the main items of food of the Harappans?

40. The Late Harappan Culture (circa 2000-1500 BC) shows a stage of de-urbanization. True or False?

41. Please write a few words on the disposal of the dead of the mature Harappans.

42. Please write a few lines on the Copper/Bronze industry of the mature Harappans.

43. Please name the Chalcolithic cultures of the north-west part of South Asia which preluded the early Harappan Chalcolithic cultures.

44. Name the culture which can be associated with the Rigvedic culture of circa 3500-2700 BC.

45. Name the village culture which can be associated with the Atharvavedic and Samavedic cultures (circa 2800-2000 BC).

46. Write the name of the sites where we get a continuous sequence from circa 8000 BC to the mature Harappan Civilization. (2700 B.C.)

47. Name a few important early Harappan sites.

48. Name a few important sites where we get a transitional stage between the early Harappan and the mature Harappan periods.

49. Name a few late Harappan sites.

50. When were wheel-made ceramics first made by South Asians?

ANSWERS:

1. (a) Alamgirpur (b) Kalibangan (c) Mohenjo-daro (d) Rangpur (e) Harappa (f) Lothal
2. 1. Yes 2. Yes 3. No
3. 1. c 2. b
4. (a) Steatite seal (b) Copper fish-hook (c) Copper mirror (d) Terracotta dice (e) Bone scale (f) Brick with footprint of a cat (g) Gold and stone bead necklace (h) Terracotta toy animal with moveable head (i) Bronze axe-adze (j) Animal-headed copper hairpin (k) Copper weighing balance and stone weights.
6. 1. Amphora 2(a) Black on red (b) Geometrical patterns, birds, animals, leaves, fish-scale and human figures.
7. 1: b, 2: c, 3: b, 4: Lost wax process i.e., first of all a figure is modelled in wax then it is covered with a coating of clay which, when dry, is heated to run out the wax. The hollow mould, thus created, is filled with molten metal, which takes the shape of the original wax figure.
8. 1: d, 2: c, 3: b, 4: Head-dress, ear ornaments, necklace, short skirt and loin cloth.
9. Across: 1. Buffalo, 6. Elephant, 8. Ram, 9. Tiger, 10. Dog, 11.Monkeys

   Down: 1. Bull, 2. Anteater, 3. Fish, 4. Rhinoceros,

   5. Squirrel, 7. Peacock
10. Bull
11. Sea-borne trade with the Persian Gulf countries

12. People worshipped mother goddess, trees and Siva-Pasupati or the lord of Animals.
13. F 1. T 2. T 3. T 4. T 5. T 6. F 7. F 8. T 9. F 10. T 11. T 12
14. 1. Pots, pans and ornaments, 2. Lothal
15. Agriculture, trade, statuary, smithy, toy making, pottery making, etc.
16. 1a. Head-dress b. Mother goddess

    2a. Harappan script b. Seal

    3a. Bangles b. Dancing girl

    4a. Necklace b. Dancing girl

    5a. Pipal leaves b. Seal
17. Unicorn
18. circa 2700-2000 BC
19. Italian scholar Lugipie Tessitori did the first excavation in 1917 at Kalibangan, a Harappan site.
20. During 1920-21 D.R. Sahani and R.D. Banerji discovered the Harappan Civilization at Harappa and Mohenjodaro.
21. Ganweriwala located on the bank of river Hakra (Gaghar or Saraswati) is the largest mature Harappan site covering an area of 250 hectares.
22. The area covered 1.6 million sq km. by the mature Harappan Civilization extended from Suktagendor, on the Makran Coast situated on the border of Iran and Pakistan, to Alamgirpur, Hulas, Mandi and Shamlinagar on Hindon in western U.P. and Shortaghai (Afghanistan) in the north to Daimabad in western Maharashtra (near Saibaba Ashram at Shiradi).

23. Early Harappan village Chalcolithic Culture and Rigvedic people were contemporary (circa 3500-2800 BC). The Mature Harappans were contemporary of Atharvavedic and Samavedic Culture and many traditions of the early Harappans continued during the mature Harappan period. The Mature Harappans were in contact with the Atharvavedic and Samavedic people and thus we can conclude the mature Harappans and Rigvedic were not the same.

24. Yes, the horse was known to the mature Harappans. Terracotta figurines of horses have been reported from Mohenjo-daro, Lothal, Banawali, Rangpur, Nausharo, Piraq and Rakhigarhi. The bone of the domestic horse was identified by A.K. Sharma at Surkotada and Kalibangan.

25. The Harappan script is on the way to decipherment. Their script was Proto Brahmi, and the direction of the Harappan writing system was mostly from right to left during the mature Harappan period and later on around c 2000-1500 B.C. their writing system was mostly from left to right, and we get such evidences from Betdwarika and Kalibangan. An inscribed double-headed terracotta human head from Kalibangan gives some clue about the script. This inscription is in the Proto Brahmi script and scholars read this inscription as SIVAM. (शिवम्) and writing is left to write.

26. Fire worship was the main ritual of the mature Harappans. They knew about yoga. The cult of Siva and Linga and Mother Goddess was an important

religion of the mature Harappans. The pipal tree was sacred for the Harappans.

27. R.D. Banerji and D.R. Sahni.

28. Around 2658 sites have been explored. 203 Harappan and its associated sites have been excavated. Mohenjo-daro, Harappa, Dholavira, Mehrgarh, Kalibangan, Lothal, Rakhigarhi, Nausharo, Banawali, are a few important sites.

29. Around 1.6 million sq. km.

30(a) Ganweriwala (250 hectares) and next comes Mehrgarh (200 hectares)

30(b) Circa 2700-2000 BC

31. Harappa in Punjab and Mohenjo-daro in Sindh both in Pakistan.

32. (a) False.

(b) True.

(c) True.

(d) Way to Decipherment.

(e) True.

33. It had the largest animal husbandry and crafts centre of the Harappan Civilization.

34. Brick, stones and wood.

35(A) Mohenjo-daro.

35(B) True.

36. Elephant, Bull, and Unicorn.

37. False (Mohenjo-daro).

38. Camel, elephant, horse and ass for land

transportation and flat-bottomed boats were used for water transportation.

39. Wheat, barley, rice, and jowar, which were supplemented by meat of cattle, buffaloes, sheep, goat, pig, rodent and chicken.

40. True.

41. The Harappan dead were usually buried in extended position with head towards the north. Some pots with or without bones were buried in pits. The Harappans were also cremating (burning) dead bodies. At Kalibangan there are evidences of different modes of disposal of the dead i.e. perhaps *'Nadipravah'* (throwing the body into the river). The Megalithic types ortho-sted type cairn circle stone monument have been reported from Surkotada and Daimabad. Rows of barrow burial of *Rath-Chiti* made of stone have been reported from Dholavira. Coffin type burials have been reported from Harappa.

42. Copper smelting furnaces, copper ingot along with melted copper and crucible for smelting have been reported from mature Harappan sites.

43. (1) Chaff Ware (circa 5550-4300 BC)

    (2) Togau Ceramics phase (circa 4300-3800 BC)

    (3) Kechi Beg ceramics phase (circa 3800-3200 BC)

    (4) Hakra ware phase (circa 3800-3200 BC)

    (5) Ravi ware phase (circa 3500-3300 BC)

    (6) Anartha culture (circa 3500-3200 BC)

44. (1) Ravi ware is the earliest deposit of Harappa (circa 3500-3300 BC)

    (2) Anartha ware culture of Gujarat (circa 3500-3000 BC)

(3) Ganeshwar culture (circa 3200-3000 BC)

(4) Balathal culture of Rajasthan (circa 3100-3000 BC)

(5) Kunal culture (circa 3200-3000 BC)

45. Copper hoard weapons and O.C.P. ceramics traditional can be associated with the Atharvavedic and Samavedic culture These traditions began around 2800 BC and continued till 1500 BC.

46. Mehrgarh and its nearby site Nausharo.

47. (1) Mehrgarh

(2) Kotdiji, Harappa

(3) Kunal

(4) Amri-Nal

(5) Kalibangan

(6) Sothi

(7) Rakhigarhi

(8) Sheri Khan Tarakai

48. (1) Kunal

(2) Kotdiji

(3) Nagwada

(4) Kalibangan

(5) Nausharo

(6) Dhalewan

49. (1) Quetta

(2) Piraq

(3) Mandi

(4) Daimabad

(5) Rangpur

(6) Bet Dwarika

(7) Cemetery H. (Harappa)

(8) Allahdino late phase.

50. Wheel made ceramics were first invented in south Asia around circa 4000-3800 B.C. by the makers of Togau ceramics ware of Mehrgarh in Baluchistan and other sites in Pakistan.

3

Stone Sculpture

Recent discoveries at the Harappan sites reveal around thirty stone statuettes from Mohenjo-daro, Harappa, Mundigak and Dholavira. The stone sculptures discovered from Mohenjo-daro, Harappa, Dholavira and Mundigak (Afghanistan) are the rarest of art objects and these art treasures can never be replenished. The maximum height of the fragmentary statuette is around 37 cm and minimum 4 cm. The discovery of stone pillars and other huge stone images from Dholavira indicates the possibilities of finding more stone sculptures from Harappan sites. For this we have to wait for extensive horizontal excavations at sites in south Asia.

A seated headless priest from Dholavira is the largest (37 cm) among the stone sculptures of Harappa. The Harappan Bronze Age urban civilization which was spread in north-western part, south Asia and southern part of Central Asia (Afghanistan & Soviet Union Border) is ascribed broadly to the period circa 2700-2000 B.C. on the basis of masca corrected carbon dates. Harappan is the earliest civilization of the Indian sub-continent and therefore any statue associated with the Harappan assumes extraordinary significance from the point of view of our cultural heritage. The Indian Harappan sites like Dhalewan, Kuntasi, Banawali, Rakhigarhi, Lothal, Kalibangan, Rohira, Surkotada etc., have not yielded any sculptures of stone except a few miniature bronze figurines.

No complete stone statues have been reported from the Indian sites except a few polished stone pillars (Lingas) and Damaru shaped calendar or *Arghya* from Dholavira (Fig. 80). It gives us an impression that we may get stone

Fig. 80 : Damaru shaped pillar

statuettes in future from the Indian sites. Harappan archaeologists must find out the reasons and explanations for such a peculiar situation in India. It has been observed that lack of extensive horizontal excavations may be the main reason for such a situation on Indian sites. During recent excavations at Dholavira three stone images have been reported. Harappa and Mohenjo-daro are situated in the nucleus region of the Harappan civilization whereas the Indian sites are on its peripheral region.

The Harappan sites situated in Pakistan and Afghanistan like Mohenjo-daro, Harappa and Mundigak have not yielded more than a dozen partly complete specimens and a dozen fragments. It highlighted the rarity of the stone statuettes and makes it doubly necessary to exercise caution. Of these stone statuettes from Pakistan, one priest-bust is now in Karachi Museum (Pakistan) and four others are in the National Museum, New Delhi. Two stone images from Dholavira of A. S.I. collection, New Delhi, are outstanding from the point of view of their artistic merit. The following are a few outstanding stone statuettes of the Harappan Civilization:

1. Male Torso (Fig. 81)
   Circa 2700 B.C. Harappa Red Stone
   Size 9´5.5´3cms, Acc. No. 9042/187
   National Museum, New Delhi.
   (D. P. Sharma: 2002)

This statue is a headless torso of a nude male and is carved out of fine-grained red colour *jaspery* sandstone. It was discovered in the excavations at Harappa. The small statue has some polish and grinding marks. This figurine was found in mound Fatehpur of Harappa, at a depth of about 1.5m below the surface. It does not have any resemblance with the stone statues of west Asia. The

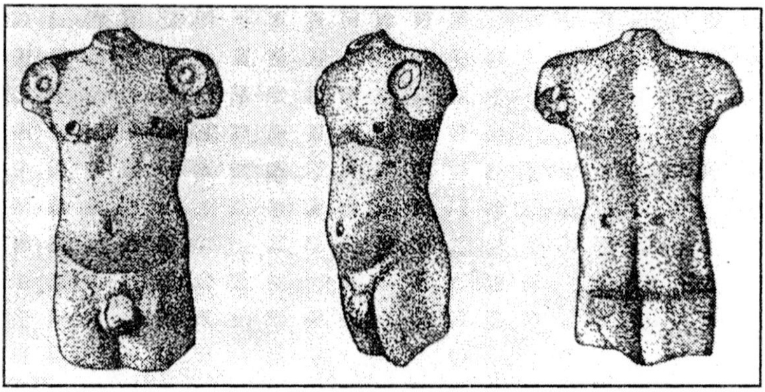

Fig. 81 : Male torso red sand stone Harappa, height 8.5 cm National Museum Collection, New Delhi

Harappans had cultural independence in style. The most striking feature of this small statue is its natural pose. The body is subtly modelled and softly contoured. The photograph of this statue without side scale, appear like a life-size figure of some well-built strongman.

Huntington observed *"Gentle transition between one part of the body of this statue and another created through sculptural means, rather than use of lines. For example, the abdominal and pectoral region smelt in three-dimensional manner and are not defined by any outline or linear demarcation. There is total absence of linear design abstract pattern, more emphasis is on the physical form of body."* From the front, the figure is static and frontal. The symmetry of the back shows the weight of the body. Sankalia observed on the basis of perfect physical form of this torso that Harappan sculptors were having mastery over human anatomy. Its beauty lies in the fact that though this figure is packed with such great anatomical details, it reflects such a high technical skill. The frontal pose of the Man looks slightly bulging. The fleshy parts of the body of this statue are noteworthy. The nudity in this figure and the depiction of the male genital portion does not indicate sexuality or fertility.

Technically, too, the polished figure is unique. Sockets are provided for the hand, the arms and nipples of the body. This technique is mainly applied for the moveable limbs. This technique was also used in a few terracotta of Harappa. Normally stone sculptures are made in one piece, but in this particular image some peculiar features of technique are seen. In this, the head, arms and nipples were made separately and added to the main torso. For affixing these parts holes were made by the craftsman in the neck, at the starting point of the arms and also on the chest. There is one more conspicuous fact i.e. each shoulder has a circular depression on the front side. The circular depression at the shoulder and neck seems to have been made with a tubular drill, which also left a small knob in the centre. These depressions seem to have been inlaid with some semi-precious stones or coloured paste which reminds of certain terracotta figurines from Baluchistan and Harappa.

This image has been compared with the torso of Jaina Tirthankara of Lohanipur (Bihar) of 3rd century B.C., which is highly polished. Both of them are made of jasper. On the basis of the resemblance of these two statues some scholars are of the opinion that this is the image of *Adinatha* the first Jaina *Thirthankara*. Some scholars have suggested that its date can go down up to the Mauryan period. In the context of the aforesaid technique, it may be added that nothing like it is discernible in the sculptures of any early historical period in India. Because of the muscularity of the figure, a Greek analogy has also been suggested. But neither the drilling technique nor the attachment of separately produced limbs is known to have not been used in case of Greek sculpture or Mauryan art. Doubts have been raised by art historians in the cases of the male torso and a stone dancer, both from Harappa, whether these two really belonged to the Harappan Civilization period i.e circa 2700-2000 B.C. This doubt emanates from the fact that even amongst the finds of the Harappan Civilization these two statuettes from Harappa are unique in technology. It was felt that these are Mauryan period statuettes and might have somehow found their way into Harappan strata. These were found at the depth of 1.5 metres at Harappa and this area has yielded nothing that is not ascribable to the Harappan Civilization. This figure is superior in aesthetic form and drilling and polishing technique to the other stone images of the Harappan Civilization. Thus the drilling and polishing techniques and craftsmanship of this figure remind us of the red Jain, a Thirthankar image of the Mauryan period from Lohanipur and a few other Greek statues of 3rd century B.C. Jasper and chalcedony are available in Schwan, Sind, Lakhi-Hills, Porali Basin, Kohistan, Ratanpur and Ranpur, all situated in the regions of Pakistan and western India.

2. Male Dancer (Fig. 82)
Circa 2700 B.C. Harappa grey stone
Size 10´4´3 cms Acc. No. 987/186
National Museum, New Delhi.
(D. P. Sharma: 2002)

The dark grey stone statue of a male dancer shown standing on his right leg and its body from the waist upwards is bent well round to the left. Both the arms are thrown in the same direction and the left leg is risen high in front. The contours of the body are soft and effeminate. According to S.

Fig. 82 : Male Dancer front view C. 2700 B.C., Harappa Grey Jesper stone. Neg No. 317-61. Acc No. 987/186. National Museum, New Delhi Collection.

R. Rao, this dancing male figure suggests perhaps the cosmic dance of Pusupati Siva. This is the earliest evidence of dancing Siva. Scholars like S.R.Rao, Sivaramamurti and Kapila Vatsyayan have called it a male dancer. The author (D.P. Sharma) has observed it as a female on the basis of the thick portions of its hips and waist and its other anatomical details of the abdominal part which give it more the appearance of a female dancer.

In this figure there is a provision for attaching limbs, which could be moved on arms. The head of this dancer has a few holes, meant for fixing heads or any other headdress, etc. A similar type of statuette in Alabaster and terracotta with provision for attaching the torso was found at Lothal and another animal-headed mother goddess terracotta at Harappa. In all these figurines limbs could have been attached. In this, the modelling of anatomical details is superb though unfortunately it is headless and armless with the broken feet below certain level. While the right leg is vertical the left one of which only the thigh is extended is thrown somewhat horizontally. Marshall had tried to reconstruct it through the drawing of the figure suggesting that it was an image of a dancer. He did not mention whether it is a male or female dancer. It is now confirmed that this is an image of a dancer. This view is partly upheld by the fact that the upper part of the body was swung towards the left and the arms too followed suit. Like the previous figure of the male torso this image too was made in pieces. The holes just below the shoulders show that the arms could have been fitted. Likewise there are holes in the upper part of the neck and on this basis Marshall concluded that there were three heads or at least three faces. Moreover it has a dancing pose. Marshall suggested that this figure may have represented youthful *Siva Nataraja*.

The other explanations of these holes is that they were meant for fixing the headdress of the dancer and one big front hole was for fixing the head of the dancer. Thus the question whether the statue is the male *Siva Nataraja* or a male dancer is still open to debate.

3. Male Head or Priest Head (Fig. 83)
   Circa 2700 B.C., Mohenjo-daro
   Limestone (white) Size 16´11.5´18.5cm
   Acc. No. HR 910/184
   National Museum, New Delhi
   (D. P. Sharma: 2002)

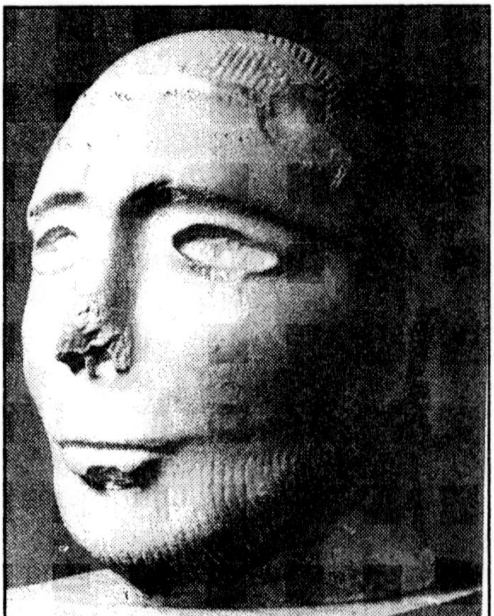

Fig. 83 : Male or Priest head. C. 2700 B.C., Mohenjodaro Neg No. 22-61, Acc No. 910/184. National Museum, New Delhi Collection.

This is a white limestone portrait head, which has a colouring of yellowish coating of steatite powder. The moustaches are almost absent in the figure though the short chin shows the prominent beard. The figure has sunken holes or oval sockets, for the almond shaped eyes which were once inlaid with semi-precious stones. The outer corners of the eyes are turned downwards (horizontal). The hair is shown cropped and held together with the fillet. The wavy hair is combed straight back and knotted in three strands into a bun held in place in the neck by a headband. A string like fillet passes around the forehead and goes back to the knot to keep it in position which is also affixed to the knot with a hairpin. The figure has stylized, shell-shaped ears. The modelling of the cheeks and the lips is sensitive. The present priest-head was discovered through excavations in southern H.R. area of Mohenjo-daro in locality House 1, Room No. 10, 2 metres below the surface. Alexandra has noticed the following important characteristics in this male head:

(1) The figure has an oval-shaped face like that of a Mongoloid head of Central Asia. Mongoloid masks (puppets) of terracotta were also reported from Mohenjo-daro and Harappa and this has been also confirmed by the discovery of a Mongoloid skeleton from the burial place Mohenjo-daro. Thus the Mongoloid elements were very well present in the Harappan population.

(2) The broad cheekbones and the receding forehead of this figure like those of the Proto Dravidian and Brahui (Baluchi) tribals are interesting.

(3) The figure has a straight nose the tip of which has been restored.

(4) The narrow upper-lip has a contrast with the thick bottom lip and the corners of the mouth are turned slightly upwards.

(5) The ears have been reduced to a simple oval shape and the auditory canal is indicated by a chiselled round hole. Alexandra and Lal have ascribed this sculpture to the late phase of Mature Harappan i.e. c 2300-2000 B.C., whereas Marshall and the author have dated it around c 2700 B.C. Marshall called it a portrait head whereas Lal is of the opinion that the "dimension of only the head portion is 16cm´15cm´18.5cm which would suggest that an attempt had been made to produce a real life-size figure like the priest king of Mohenjo-daro and they

noticed that this figure does not have any polish at all. If this head is a kind of portrait as Marshall thought, then we must have here indication of the physical feature of a person, at least of some of them who constituted the Harappan population".

The most unique feature in this figure is two eyes, which have long horizontal eyelids with the inner and outer corners horizontally opposed. When this head was discovered, one shell inlay was fixed to the left eye. The horizontal position and the half-closed eye remind us of the typical characteristic of the eye of the Gupta period Buddha which indicated that this head is in an attitude of meditation. The naturalistic ears were made with the help of shell ornaments, which appear like the abstract reproduction of a helix ear shape. Shell ornaments were also discovered from Mohenjo-daro.

The common denominator of the art style of Harappan stone sculpture is the socketted eye with an inlay work of paste, gems, semi-precious stone, shell, etc., which are a typical characteristic of the Harappan art style. The shell-shaped human ears are typical of the Mature Harappan art. The hairstyle of these sculptures is parallel to the style of the stone sculptures from Helmand region like Mundigak IV 3, Tape Yalya IV B, Sahri-Sokta and various other sites in Seistan and west Asia (Mesopotamia and Egypt). Big tail type hair dress is a unique characteristic of Harappan images. The round bun type hair dress on the back of the head is typically indigenous and resembles with the proto Dravidian style of Tamil Nadu, especially the dancer of *Bharat-Natayam* which shows a continuous tradition from the dancing girl of Mohenjo-daro to the present day dancer. This hairstyle was also prevailing in the arts of Chola and Pallava periods, which fact is clear from their sculptures in bronze and stone of Tamil Nadu.

The two plaits of hair at the back of the Harappan head is a typical west Asian style and this we also notice in the hair style of the priest king bust from Mohenjo-daro. The shell inlay pieces of ears, eyes and kidney and various other shapes, which were discovered along with these stone sculptures, might have been used for inlaying semi-precious-stones, ivory and shell ornaments.

It is noteworthy that around twenty stone sculptures of Harappan Civilization have been described in which fourteen are of male and the remaining fragmentary ones belong to the animal world. It is also to be noted that not a single female stone sculpture was reported from any Harappan site except a headless figure of a dancer or a female dancer, if we accept this as a female dancer. This large number of male figures also contradicts the earlier view of scholars that females were dominant in the Harappan society.

A large number of ring stones, pully-shaped circular stones cylindrical pillars with mushroom type head on top, circular bases of pillars and other components of pillar which have some polish or grinding were reported from Mohenjo-daro, Harappa and Dholavira. Some scholars have identified these as calendar stones while others have called them as pillar bases of stone probably used for gates / doors, etc., of the citadel. A few of these Ring Stones which have wide circular holes along with a conical stone phallus were associated with *Siva Lingam* whereas others with some markings and holes on their sides and top were called calendar stones. A few head-shaped pillars resembling in art style with the Doric (Greek) style of famous Heliodorus pillar at Vidisha (M.P.) and Menander (Posthumous) pillar at Reh district Fatehpur (U.P.) are either *Siva Lingam* or related with the solar watch by which the Harappan people were measuring time. These polished sandstone pillars are now exhibited in the site museums of Harappa, Mohenjo-daro and Dholavira, National Museums of Karachi and New Delhi and also in the Prince of Wales Museum Mumbai. Scholars have interpreted these polished stone objects commonly called the great ring stones or *Yoni* stones, great wavy ring stones, *Linga* stones, cones and bagle like stones, pillar bases or pillar components and also astronomical calendar or sun-watch. These objects are of various shapes like those of the ring, mace head, solid wheel, pulley, cylinder with a small hole in the middle (Pillar base) and cylindrical pillar hood, and range in height form 3'-4' to 6'. The excavator of Dholavira, R. S. Bisht, is of the opinion that at Mohenjo-daro and Harappa the circular ring stones were interpreted as *Yoni* (Phallus) and *Arghya* and the pillars were interpreted as *Siva Lingam* or Calendar Stones. But the recent discoveries of similar type of polished round stones with short cylindrical mouths show that they were used in the construction of some structure, particularly pillars with capitals. (Fig. 84)

Fig. 84 : Stone pillar fragment, Dholavira, C. 2600-2000 B.C.

Elizabeth has recently observed that those great ring stones are not calendar stones. The excavation at Room No.49 of H.R. area of Mohenjo-daro indicates that they could have been stored by piling them up and then securing them with a wooden pole, thus ensuring that the topmost part of it does not slide off. Perhaps the square and round-topped capitals or hood shaped terminals found along with them might have been fixed on the top. She opines that these pillars with hood shaped tops are not representations of the Phallic symbol of *Yoni*. These are highly polished or smoothed stone pillars of 4' to 6' in height with the top looking like a *Mushroom*, which the excavator of Dholavira found standing amidst the large buildings near the eastern fortification wall. However, the present author (D.P. Sharma) has observed that these hood shaped 6 feet high pillars resemble the pillar fragment of Reh, which belongs to the Indo-Greek king Menander (Posthumous). The excavator of Dholavira feels that these pillars were purely of decorative purposes, a system which the Greek adopted some 2500 years later. The above conclusion of Bisht has not yet been accepted. The purpose of the hood-shaped pillars is still not clear.

Round and rectangular components well ground as well as superbly smoothed of stone pillars have been discovered in a large quantity at Dholavira. The explanation of these pillar base components as parts of pillars is quite possible. However, the present author (D.P. Sharma) is of the opinion that they were securing them with solid copper rods in the middle or with wood. This explanation fits well with the pillar bases of Dholavira. Thus we can presume that these are components of pillars and the hood-shaped component might be the top portion of this pillar.

A few pulley-shaped solid wheel type polished ring stones might have been used as pulleys. These pulleys were fixed on the top of these pillar components and these were used for opening and closing the door or entrance. The solid wheel-shaped pulleys reported from Dholavira, Harappa and Mohenjo-daro seem to be components of the door of a citadel as these were discovered near the gate of the citadel area.

4

Bronze Figurines

Around one dozen bronze statues and three-dozen miniature bronze figurines were reported from the mature phase of various Harappan sites. Besides this, four heavy bronze sculptures of the late Harappan period were discovered by chance discovery from Daimabad later, on the stratified deposits of the late Harappan period which were also confirmed at the find spot of these bronzes. It is interesting to note that the total number of bronze images yielded at the Harappan sites is even lesser than the stone sculpture and terracotta figurines. From the point of view of artistic merit as well as technique these stand out on their own right. Here only a few specimens that are extremely remarkable in the mature Harappan period are described below:

1. Dancing Girl (Fig. 85-86)
   Circa 2700 B.C., Mohenjodaro
   Bronze Size 10.5 ´ 5 ´ 2.5cms
   Acc. No. HR 5721/195
   National Museum, New Delhi
   (D. P. Sharma: 2002)

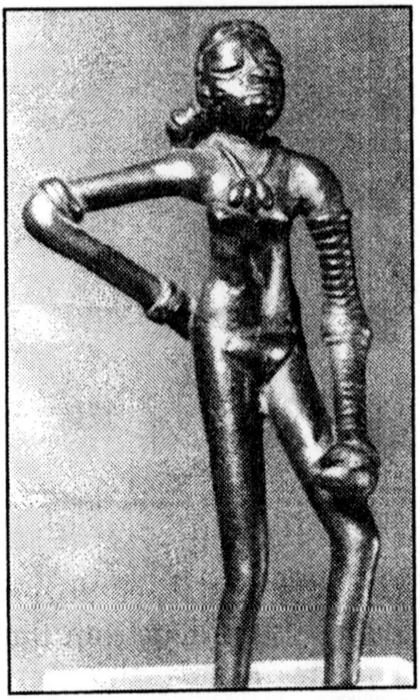

Fig. 85 : Dancing girl, C. 2700 B.C., Mohenjodaro Bronze, Neg No. 330-61, Acc No. Hr 5721/195, National Museum, New Delhi Collection.

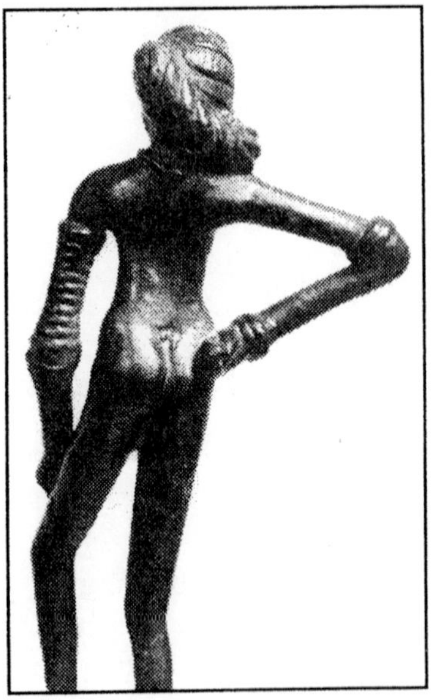

Fig. 86 : Dancing girl C. 2700 B.C., Mohenjodaro Bronze, Neg. No. 144-61. Acc No. Hr 5721/195. National Museum, New Delhi Collection.

Two bronze dancing girls were discovered through early excavations done by Marshall (1931) at Mohenjo-daro in which one superb example is now in exhibition at the Harappan gallery of the National Museum, New Delhi, and another one which is crude and unfinished is now in the collection of the National Museum of Karachi. Both have arsenic contents as a mixture of Bronze and appear like Proto Dravidian tribal girls in appearance. The Dancing Girl exhibited in the National Museum, New Delhi, is the finest and most superb and is un-surpassed in art style among all the bronze figurines so far discovered from the Harappan sites. This figurine is one of the highest achievements of the metal artist of Harappan Civilization. The right hand of this figure rests on the hip, the left arm covered almost entirely with bangles, hangs loosely and seems relaxing by the posture of legs. It appears, she is taking some rest after a long dance performance. The bangles on one hand reminds us that she was probably a follower of *Murugan (Son of Siva) or Rudra Siva* god and she might have performed her dance in the *Rudra or Siva* Temple. The modelling of the back, hips and buttocks, evidenced in a small figure as this is quite effective. She is nude but her necklace is decorated with three beads and a similar type of necklaces made of carnelian and agate beads were discovered through excavations at Mohenjo-daro, which are now displayed in the exhibition of the Jewellery gallery of the National Museum, New Delhi, and an identical necklace in the collection of Karachi Museum, Pakistan. The hair of this figure is plaited in an elaborate manner. True to the above facts the arms and legs are disproportionately elongated. This bronze figure was cast by the *cire perdue* or lost wax solid cast process. This bronze figure is easily amongst the most publicized objects of the Harappan Civilization and this is rarest among all the art objects of South Asia. Her over burdened ornaments are interesting which divert the attention of her nudity. The head is slightly drawn backwards with its eye semi-open, which gives the impression of her dancing pose.

The tribal head of this figure is provocatively tilted and gives the impression of a *Proto Dravidian* tribal girl. The large eyes, flat nose and head and bunched curly hair remind us of a *Tribal Dravidian* girl. In ancient times of Chola period in Tamil Nadu around four hundred women were serving as temple dancers. Dancing in the Dravidian temples of south India is still popular, which is performed by dancing girls *(Devadasi)*, which reflects a continuous tradition and legacy of *Proto Dravidian* i.e. Harappan people in the Dravidian language speaking region of South India. Dances are still performed by these female *Devadasi* dancers at the Drasavam Temple of Tanjore in Madras. The *Karama*

Vinithi dance festival still prevails among the girls of Santhal and Bihar who associate them with *Sapta Sindhu*. The Santhal tribe also speaks Dravidian words. Various dance styles like the *Bharat Natyam*, etc., prevalent in South India since Sangam age through Chola period and also in modern period. Various dancing poses of *Siva Nataraja* of Chola period in the Dravidian region of South India and the slender feminine figure also reminds us of the continuous dancing tradition of the dancing girl of the Harappan Civilization. A few jewellery items like *Rudraksa Mala*, Sun and Moon worn by the present day dancer of *Bharat Natyam* resemble the jewellery items of the Harappan Civilization and show the continuous tradition of the Harappan's dance among the present day Dravidian of South India.

It is interesting to note that in North India only a few dance styles like *Kathak, Dandiya*, etc., prevail and these styles became popular in India during post 12th century A.D. and their beginning can be traced back to the *Mahabharat* period whereas in South India there is a variety in the dance style like the *Bharat-Natyam, Katha Kali, Kuchipudi, Mohani Attam, etc.*, which shows a continuous tradition of the dance of *Proto Dravidian* i.e. the Harappan people who later on during post Harappan period shifted to the Dravidian region of South India through the western coast of India. However, we need some more evidence to prove this theory of migration. A recent discovery of Megalithic material from the Deccan datable C. 1600-1000 B.C. shows the Harappan legacy.

A kind of haughtiness reign over her face and its hair-do style resembles that of a *Bharat Natyam* dancer of the Dravidian region in South India and also the hairstyle between Chola bronze and the sculptures of South India. It is interesting to note here that the *Bharat Natyam* is the earliest known dance tradition of the Dravidian language speaking people of South India. The figure of the dancing girl is the earliest evidence of dance and also the female metal image of India, perhaps in the whole world. Besides this, there is one more dancing torso of stone from Harappa. On the basis of the discovery of these three dance sculptures of the Harappan Civilization, we may conclude that dancing was an important item for recreation and entertainment of the Harappan Civilization. This small piece in dancing is most remarkable of early Indian art and its casting technique is also noteworthy.

Besides this figurine there is another blurred, crude, unfinished bronze dancing girl from Mohenjo-daro now exhibited in Karachi Museum, Pakistan. The facial expression of this figure is not clear. The left hand of this figurine is on her private parts and the right on her hips. The art style and finishing technique is crude and seems to be partly unfinished. The height of this figure is 13 cm. Other fragmentary pieces of Bronzes from Mohenjo-daro, which are also related to dance, are a miniature female dancer (height 4.1 cm) and bronze feet portion of female dancer (height 2.9 cm). All these finds confirm that dancing was an integral part of Harappan society and dance was an important item of entertainment.

2. Buffalo (Fig. 87) Bronze
   Circa 2700 B.C., Mohenjo-daro
   Size 7.5 ´ 3.5 cms Acc. No. 3319/1046
   National Museum, New Delhi
   (D. P. Sharma: 2002)

This small solid cast bronze buffalo of a well-built muscular body type is a unique example of the solid bronze casting technique of the Harappans. A strong animal is standing in a very interesting manner. The head of the buffalo is slightly turned to the right in a mixed attitude of

Fig. 87 : Buffalo, Bronze ACC No. 3319/1046 National Museum, New Delhi

defence and vigilance. Indeed it is a most realistic and powerful rendering of a buffalo and hence it is unique and of consequent importance. Its two horns are alert for action while facing danger and the lashing curved tail shows that the suspected danger is over. A similar type of bronze bull or buffalo was also reported from Kalibangan, which is now in the collection of the National Museum, New Delhi. In both the figurines the posture as well as modelling are marked by the careful handling of the body contour and rolling mass of flesh of the body. Possibly the greatest achievement of the sculpture lies in the fact that the artist has succeeded in infusing the figure with the sap of life and the delicate feeling of the pet animal and also capturing a moment of repose in its life.

Besides these above two figurines the National Museum, New Delhi, also has a very small figurine of a buffalo from Mohenjo-daro, which was sent to the exhibitions of Berlin and Florence. The above bronze figurines of two buffaloes and a bull were prepared by the cire-perdue or solid cast lost method. Some of these bronzes were examined and have arsenic contents. These figurines suffered badly from corrosion and the surface is extremely pitted. The other small bronze of a buffalo measuring 3.1x5.7x1.7 cm was discovered from Mohenjo-daro at the depth of 2' 1 1" below the surface. This miniature superb bonze statue testifies to the sympathic interest that the Harappan artist had in depicting nature and his ability to capture the intrinsic life of its forms. The neck portion of this figure is heavy, supported by strong legs. One miniature copper duck and a dog from Lothal, a miniature dog from Mohenjo-daro and a Rabbit from Dholavira are also interesting. A few polished mirrors with handle of copper from Dholavira, Harappa, Mehi, Kalibangan, Lothal, Shortaghai Mohenjo-daro and Rakhigarhi are of special artistic merit. These seem to be toiletry items.

Besides the above mentioned copper-bronze image of Harappans, other copper/bronze miniature figurines are models of a short horned bull, a model of a couchant goat on a stamp (Ht.5.4 cm), a model of a couchant ram (Ht.3.25 cm), an antelope or a gazelle-all from Mohenjo-daro a copper dog from Mohenjo-daro and these are now exhibited in Mohenjo-daro site Museum and the National Museum, New Delhi. Other noteworthy copper ornaments or objects of the Harappan Civilization are: a lid with stems radiating from a centre which has an upright bar capped by a buffalo figure (Ht. 14 cm) from Mohenjo-daro, a vessel lid with twelve curve stem radiating two animals (Bull or mythical horse) and chariot driven by a man from Mohenjo-daro and Daimabad. The facial expression of this standing charioteer (man) appears like that of a *Proto Austroloid.*

5

Terracotta Figurines

The terracotta figurines of the Harappan Civilization are mostly hand made and only a few are mould/wheel made. After the clay modelling red or cream slip or wash was applied on these figurines. These clay figurines were fired at a very high temperature in reducing condition i.e. in closed furnace. The Colour of the core is mostly red. In some cases it is black. The female terracotta figurines out number the male figurines and on this basis we can conclude that Harappan Society was female-dominated. The female terracotta figurines of the Harappan Civilization have thin waists, conical bare breasts and broad hips, with a loincloth and a girdle and are adorned with a series of necklaces and head ornaments. The over-burdened decorated female figurines were regarded as mother-goddesses. The male figurines are less elaborate and a few masks are mould-made. The masks have a small goat like beard and long horns. The tiny male-head and an inscribed double-headed human figure and *Siva linga with Arghya* from Kalibangan are noteworthy. A few seated male figurines in *Yogasana* from Harappa confirm that the

Harappans knew *Yoga*. Some other standing male figurines from the Harappan sites are completely nude and a few of them have cut marks on the sexual organ. It confirms that religious rite was prevalent among the Harappans. A similar rite is still being performed by the present day Muslims of Asia. Among the terracotta animal figurines the bull is dominant. The bull without the hump from Mohenjo-daro and Kalibangan, the bull with a moveable head from Mohenjo-daro, a climbing monkey and a unicorn from Chanhudaro and Dholavira, etc., are of special attraction. A man holding a duck, a mythical bird with wheel, a bird in cage, a peacock and a hen are of unique artistic value.

Male Terracotta Figurines

Human terracotta figurines from the mature Harappan sites are mostly solid but a few masks are hollow. Male figures are found in large numbers in Harappa but at Mohenjo-daro female figures are dominated. This gives an impression that Mohenjo-daro was a female-dominated urban city whereas Harappa was dominated by the male population as here male figurines are one-third of the total collection. The Harappan sites like Kalibangan, Lothal and Rakhigarhi have very few human figurines but Dholavira and Banawali sites yielded some typical bird faces and Jain Thirthankar type female figurines showing richly decorated hairstyle and peculiar girdle. Those resemble the figurines of Mehrgarh and Sheri-khan-Tarakai. The human figurines recovered from Kalibangan, Lothal, Dholavira, Rakhigarhi and Banawali are very primitive in appearance and are without ornaments and decoration. The nude male forms are mostly seated with arms either on or around the knees or joined in front in devotion and *yogic* postures. In some cases legs are squatted on haunches. There are a few standing nude male terracottas with a pinched nose, either clean-shaven or bearded. The appearance is crude and rough. The male terracotta figurines from Mohenjo-daro, Harappa etc., have a short square curbed beard. The Harappa terracotta figurines were cast with a high collar and conical cap but the Mohenjo-daro figurines show cap or turban. The horned male wears turban or hair tied in a spiral cone. The male figurines from Kalibangan have more realistic eyes made of holes, pinched nose, low forehead, thick lips, prominent chin and shaven head.

The Chanhudaro terracotta figurines are solid. Male figurines were also reported from Nausharo (Pakistan). A double-faced human head from Kalibangan is of unique artistic value. This is mould-made and resembles the west Asian-art style. There are very few fragmentary human figurines from Dholavira. But females and animals (Bull) are in large numbers. Other interesting figurines are a mummy, a model of African gorilla both from Lothal. At Banawali and Dholavira female and animal figurines occur in large numbers. On the basis of the discovery of terracotta figurines at Banawali and Dholavira where female figurines are far more, we can conclude that these two cities also were female-dominated urban centres. Around 1000 terracotta figurines were reported from Rakhigarhi. The new excavation at Dhalewan yielded 50 terracotta figurines. Some interesting mould-made terracotta masks (Puppet) and male figurines are described below:

1 Human mask Terracotta (Fig. 88).
C-2700-2000 B.C., Mohenjo-daro, Pakistan,
Size 8´6.5´5 cm Acc. No. D.K 13013/248
Neg. No. 3443-88.
National Museum, New Delhi
(D. P. Sharma: 2002)

The chocolate-coloured human hollow mask (Puppet) is an outstanding example of Harappan terracotta art. This

Fig. 88 : Human mask or puppet, mould made. C. 2700-2000 B.C. Mohenjodaro, Terracotta. Neg No. 3443-88, Acc No. DK. 13013/248. National Museum, New Delhi Collection.

is unique because ninety-eight per cent of the terracotta figurines from Harappan sites are handmade. An open clay mould was also discovered in the excavation at Mohenjo-daro, which indicates that these masks were prepared by the open mould method at the site itself. The figurine is rough with traces of grey or chocolate slip and is moderately baked. The back portion is hollow and the extra clay was not removed from its edges. The two horns and ears are partly broken and the beard is gathered and tied in a flat knot. The figure has two side holes apparently meant for tying a thread. The facial portion is elongated with slight depressions near the outer corner of the eyes. The slanting eyes of this figure are concave and there is less space between the eye ridge and eye ball, and the eyes were carefully touched up. The nose is elongated and thick near the nostrils. The mouth portion is comparatively smaller and the lips are curved. There is a cut mark on the right cheek.

The number of terracotta masks discovered from Nausharo, Mohenjo-daro, Kalibangan, Harappa and other (Harappan) sites are meagre and all such masks were prepared by a single open mould. The mask might have served for decoration on some wooden structure perhaps fastened to the doors or walls of the house to avert ill-luck.

Some other scholars are of the opinion that masks were used for some magic or ritual purposes. D.P. Sharma and A.K. Das are of the opinion that the mask was probably used as the face of a puppet and the body part of the puppet was made of cloth and wood or any other soft material. The two side holes and lugs might have been served for threading. A puppet master generally uses thread for operating his puppets. This is the earliest available evidence of puppets in South Asia.

The hollow masks reported from the Harappan sites suggest that these were intended to be attached to some objects possibly a kind of doll. The mask under discussion resembles a few other masks from the Harappan sites, such as the one-horned mask from Mohenjodaro (Acc No. D.K. 9208/250), another huge mask from Mohenjo-daro reported by Dale (1986), one small mask from Mohenjo-daro now exhibited in the National Museum of Karachi (N.M.K. 50. 772), a lion mask from Mohenjo-daro (D.K. 2380B), a human mask from Mohenjo-daro now in Mohenjo-daro Museum, (D.K. 12166/830) other two from Mohenjo-daro now one in the collection of National Museum of Karachi (D.K. 8857/50.550), another one in the National Museum, New Delhi. (E 958/284) (Fig. 89).

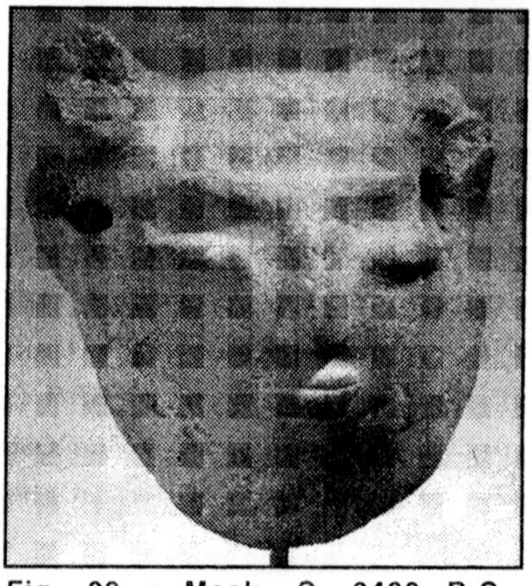

Fig. 89 : Mask, C. 2400 B.C., Mohenjodaro Terracotta, Neg No. 3937-88, National Museum, New Delhi Collection.

The almond-shaped eyes of this mask suggests the presence of a people of ethnic group from the region now known as Mongolia. The mouth is small and the lips are thick. The face of this figure resembles that of the second bronze dancing girl from Mohenjo-daro which is now in the National Museum of Karachi. The facial expression of this mask and the dancing girl can be described as *watered down*. These figurines have very shallow slanting eyes and a long straight nose. The above-mentioned bronze gives a very magnificent appearance. This terracotta figure has a short beard and its terminal point projects slightly outwards as observed in Egyptian images. A similar type of beard was noticed in two other terracotta masks and in a sculpture of stone from Mohenjodaro and also on some seals especially the one which shows a tree with a tiger below. The mask under discussion was found in the upper level of Mohenjo-daro and this can be dated between circa 2400 to 2200 B.C.

Other details like horns and ears are hand-made and joined at a later stage when the head was being prepared by mould and the clay was soft to take a firm grip for fixing separate horns and also ears and perforation of a hole. The lugs on the two sides were also made during this stage. The face of this figure was shaped by pressing out clay lying against the open mould. The excess of the pressed clay is still visible at the top and middle of the back portion of the mask. This is a rough mould-made mask.

E.C.L. During-Caspers writes, "These masks may have served to ornament of some wooden structure, as did the metal heads on a chariot found at Ur. Perhaps these were fastened to the doors on walls of houses to avert ill luck like the Burcrania used for this purpose. The Horns found on these masks suggest these were also used in some ritual dance. The dancer found in some of the rock paintings of Europe and also in present day tribal ritual dances and ceremonies in some parts of India, adorns similar horns. D.P. Sharma is of the opinion that horn figurines and masks may represent deities. In fact these masks represent magic hunting concepts. The Mongolian features copulated in the horned masks is not accidental and may well mark the presence of a minority ethnic group at Mohenjo-daro of non-Harappan inhabitants whose original home land was in Afghanistan, Kashmir, South-Tulkeman (South of USSR) or Mongolia. The practice of hunting, magic and sorcery attuned to the catching of large game still existed in the more remote areas of the Harappan region. It is very interesting to note that these masks indicate the presence of a Mongolian ethnic group and recalls the horned figure on two of the edges of a seal (RN 356) which have been likened to the hero Enkidu who appears so frequently on the Sumerian seal (RI 52 a) now in Pakistan. According to Mackay the masks found at the lower level of Mohenjo-daro are very different in technique. The early examples of lower level have very oblong Mongolian eyes which are very carefully touched. The eyes are elongated like the Buddha's down-cast eyes in the Gupta period images and undoubtedly superior in their workmanship and can readily be distinguished from the masks of a later date. On the basis of the eyes and other particulars these masks can be classified in two groups, one is slanting eyes and the other fully open eyes like the eyes of the Buddha of Mathura art of the Kushan period. These figures wear no headdress or hair style and this mask does not have any central figure over the head. The horns of this figure are smooth, unribbed and angled like those of the short horned bull.

The Harappan clay art as a whole bears an unexplained crudeness, clumsiness and seemingly lack of creative capacity. The clay artist's mode of expression was possibly governed by unwritten rules. The artists of the Harappan civilizations were familiar with the use of open as well as close mould and also with the cire-perdue process which were employed in the production of copper tablets and bronze figures. A similar head stone was also reported at Tell-Asmar, a pre Surgonid period site in West-Asia. One open clay mould of a bull head was discovered in the 1964-65 excavation of Mohenjo-daro conducted by G.F. Dales, which confirms that the mature Harappan had used mould for the preparation of terracottas.

2. Male Head (Fig. 90). Terracotta,
Circa 2700-2100 B.C., Kalibangan,
Ht. 1" Acc. No. L. 366 Loan from A.S.I.
Neg. No. R 3398 & 3399 and 1987-95
National Museum, New Delhi.

This outstanding terracotta is a small solid head and the neck portion is elongated and has some incision marks. The nose is short and has more space between the tip of the nose and lips. The two eye balls are marked by the pinching method. There is some depression between the eye brow and eye pellet. The fore-head is short and has carved lines on the top. The facial expression of this figure resembles the faces of two other bronze male charioteers- one from Daimabad and another from Mohenjodaro-and also with the face of two bronze dancing girls from Mohenjo-daro. The head also resembles the two other male terracotta heads from Kalibangan which are now in the collection of National Museum, of India (Fig. 91).

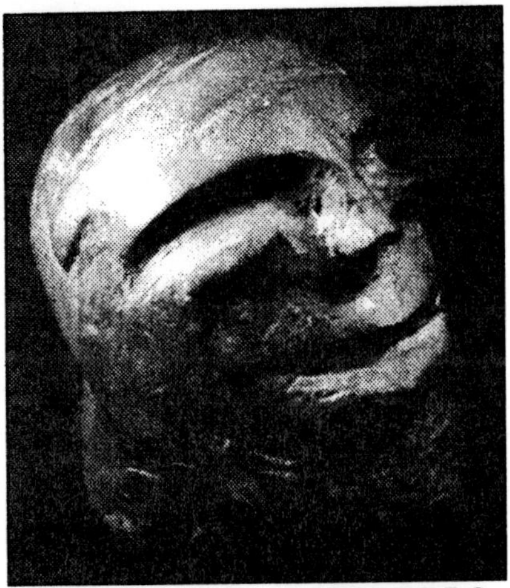

Fig. 90 : Male Head, C. 2700-2000 B.C., Kalibangan, Terracotta. Neg No. R3400, Acc No. L366. National Museum, New Delhi Collection.

The figurine is hand-modelled and the facial details were made by the pinching and incised method. In this figurine the artist has modelled the true form of an ethnic male head. This is a rare figurine which represents the Anthropomorphic form of the Harappan people. The figurine under discussion was found through excavation at Kalibangan. This male head represents the ethnic group which existed during the mature Harappan times. This object was included in the exhibition organized by the National Museum of India during WAC III 1994.

Fig. 91 : Male heads, C. 2600-2000 B.C., Kalibangan, Terracotta Neg No. 685-97, National Museum New Delhi Collection.

3. Double-Headed human figurine
Circa 2300-2000 B.C., Kalibangan
Terracotta (Fig. 92) (a&b) Size 4.5 ´ 4 cm
Neg. No. 83-95, Loan from A.S. I.
Reg. No. 295. K L B x 17)
National Museum, New Delhi.
(Sharma D.P. 2002)

This mould-made double headed male figurine was discovered through the excavation of Kalibangan. The eyes are marked by a hole, mouth, etc., and were prepared by the pinching method. The Taurine or proto-type of *Nandipada graffiti* marks are engraved on its forehead. Besides this, there are few other graffiti marks *like early Brahmi Sa type sign*. Artistically the figurine is crude. Below

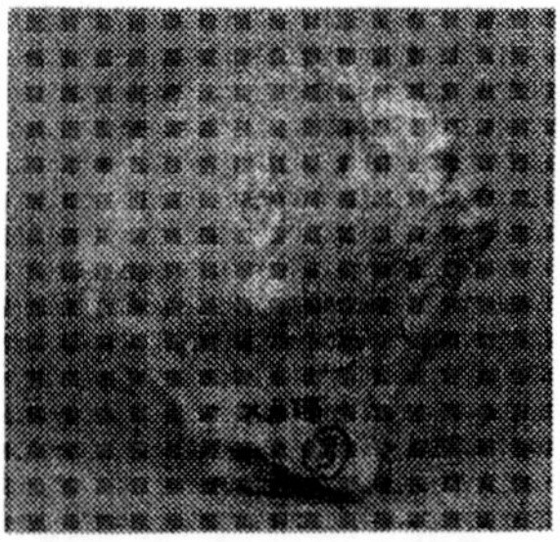

Fig. 92a

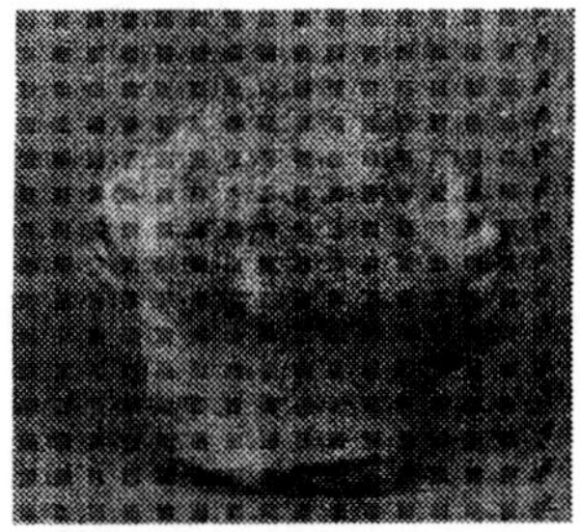

Fig. 92b

the Taurine symbol there is a third graffiti mark which appears like Brahmi *Ma or Va.* 𑀯 The details of the graffiti mark on this head are as follows : 𑀰𑀺𑀯𑀫

The graffiti marks as a whole can be read in Proto Brahmi script as **शिवम्** or Shivam.

On the basis of this proto-Brahmi inscription or late Indus graffiti marks this figure can be called a double-headed SIVA. We may conclude that the Harappan script was perhaps Proto Brahmi and its languages were *Laukik Sanskrit & Brahui.* A few proto Brahmi type graffiti marks were also discovered on pots of late Harappan (c 1600 B.C.) from Bet Dwarika which gives us thought that the Brahmi script of 6th (C. B.C.) has its origin from the proto-Brahmi script of the late Mature Harappan. (C. 2000 B.C.)

4 Seated male in *Namaskar* pose. Terracotta (Fig. 93)
Circa 2700-2100 B.C., Harappa
Size 5´4´2 cm Acc. No. 3072/388
National Museum, New Delhi.
(D. P. Sharma: 2002)

M.S. Vatsa had found this cream coloured, hand-modelled male nude figurine through the excavation at Harappa. The seated male is in *Yogic* posture with legs outstretched and knees slightly raised. The head and folded hands are in *Namaskar Mudra.* Some parts of the feet are missing. The head, mouth and nose are pinched and the two eyes are marked by round pellets. The fingers are not

Fig. 93 : Male seated in yogic posture (Mature Harappan), Harappa, C. 2700 B.C. National Museum New Delhi Collection.

marked in hands. The figurine is thin and flat but the triangular forehead is pinched at two sides. The facial expression of this figure is not clear. The well-preserved long arms of this squatting male reveals the clasped hands in devotional or *Yogic* pose. This type of *yogic* pose in male figures is rarely found in Indian art. The Harappan terracotta figurines lack the traditional embellishment of costume, ornaments and headdress but its facial features were modelled in the crude hand-made Harappan style.

Around ten *Yogic* nude human figurines have been reported from Harappa (Vatsa XXVI 1-10). The nude male figurines of the Harappan sites are commonly found seated and the legs are doubled underneath. Seven such figurines from Harappa are in *Namaskar* pose.

It is interesting to note that seated *yogic* human figurines are rare at Mohenjo-daro. This is the earliest evidence of *Yoga* scene in Indian art.

The figurine under discussion was displayed in the exhibition of 4000 years of Indian Terracotta Art which was held in 1986 in the Brooklyn Museum in U.S.A.

Female Terracotta Figurines

A large number of female terracotta figurines were discovered from sites, viz., Mohenjo-daro, Harappa and Chanhudaro all in Pakistan now. But the yield of similar objects from the Harappan sites in India is very meagre, a phenomenon which remains unexplained. The appearance and method of making these figurines are solid, hand-made and crude in art style.

Symbolism : Many of these figurines represent the mother goddess of the fertility cult. These objects are invariably presented with broad hips and heavy ornamentation. The Hermaphrodite representation on terracotta figurines from Sheri Khan Tarakai also represents the fertility cult. Similarly, triangular terracotta cakes reported from various early and mature Harappan sites are symbolic representations of mother goddesses. It is interesting to note that the earliest evidence of this cult in India was discovered from Belan valley in Allahabad. It is a very small object of bone and is dated by C^{14} method to c. 18000 B.C.

Around fourty-five terracotta female figurines were discovered through excavations from the various Harappan sites in India. These include two standing female figurines from Lothal, a few from Kalibangan, 16 from Banawali, 9 headless standing nude Jain Thirthankar type figurines from Dholavira and some heads from Rakhigarhi and Dhalewan. The female terracotta figurines from Indian sites have very little decoration and resemble in art style with the early-Harappan female terracottas and pot belly females with a beak like nose, and two decorated mother goddesses from Banawali show some similarities in art style with the mother goddess of Harappa and Mohenjo-daro. The two headless female figurines from Dholavira are unique and very different from the Harappan and early Harappan female terracotta art. Their art style resembles the West Asian (Iran). All the female terracotta figurines from Indian sites are hand-made whereas some hollow animal heads and human heads from Kalibangan were prepared by the single mould.

These terracotta figurines prove very revealing as far as the physical characteristics, dress, ornamentation and the work involvement of the Harappan females were concerned. They are shown going about with bare breasts-conical in shape. The hips are broad and the waists slender. The upper part of the body is generally devoid of any clothing but the lower part is covered with a garment resembling a mini-skirt. A turban or cloth wrap is shown round the head. The head ornaments are more ornate and elaborate. The Harappan females were very fond of jewellery as is evident from the variety of designs. Practically every part of the body was adorned with ornaments, such as multiple necklaces, made of plain strips or long chains, beads, pendants, ear-rings, bracelets, bangles, etc. Jewellery in gold and silver was also found through the excavations. These figurines present scenes from the daily life of a woman doing a variety of domestic works, such as kneading dough, baking bread, carrying baskets full of bread, nursing, feeding infants, etc.

Some of the figurines are having a coating of faience. The figurines were made by employing the applique method and pinching the clay for bringing out various facial details and body parts.

The following are a few important female terracottas from mature Harappan period:

5. Standing Tall Mother goddess. Terracotta (Fig. 94)
   Circa 2700-2100 B.C., Mohenjo-daro
   Size 23´8.5´4.0 cm Neg. No. 16-78
   Acc. No. D.K. 3506/260
   National Museum, New Delhi

One of the most outstanding terracottas of the Indus valley is a large size female figurine from Mohenjo-daro

Fig. 94 : Standing tall mother goddess C. 2700-2000 B.C. Mohenjodaro, Terracotta, Neg No. 16-78, Acc No. DK 3506/260, National Museum New Delhi Collection.

which is now on display in the Harappan gallery of the National Museum, New Delhi. This is a rare and very elaborate piece. There are 40 terracotta female figurines in the total collection of the National Museum, which were acquired through the excavations from Harappa, Mohenjo-daro and other Harappan sites. The height of this figurine is 23 cms. and it stands tallest amongst all other female figurines in the collection of the National Museum. This female figurine was discovered by Mackay through the excavation at the D.K. area of Mohenjo-daro. The figurine is hand-made and has a coating of thick red slip ! It is interesting to note that only a few female figurines have been reported from Dholavira and Banawali-both Harappan sites situated in the Indian region. This figurine is adorned with the peculiar fan shaped head-dress. The large panniers-cups like objects-are suspended on either side of the head. The cup portion has some black colour impression of charcoal and most probably these were used for burning oil or incense. The pannier-like objects are visible in almost all the female figurines of the Harappan sites. In some other figurines the panniers are large and deep. Another similar figurine from Mohenjo-daro (Marshall, 1931 plate VI) has this attachment on one side only. In other female figurines the two panniers are supported by a band carried around the head which suggests that these were attached in some way to the ears.

This figurine is wearing cone type objects on the forehead which resembles the hollow conical headdress object of gold found from the jewellery hoard of Mohenjo-daro and other sites. Similar hollow conical metal objects are still in use by the females of Nagaur in North Rajasthan suggesting continuity of tradation from the Harappan times. The female figurines have two broken unidentified conical objects near either sides of the head, just below the two panniers. According to Marshall, "this curious cone on each side of the face is really a part of the headdress and affixed to the face are perhaps two corners of the coil. On the other hand, an ornament of some kind may have been attached to the coil and, if so, this shape recalls the hollow gold cone which was found with the other jewellery in the D.K. Area and illustrated in plate CXLVII. The gold cone of the jewellery from Mohenjo-daro has a loop inside the apex presumably for sewing on to a garment. A very similar ornament made of faience has been found from Mohenjo-daro and Dholavira and this also has a loop inside for attachment to the clothing.

The figurine does not have upper garments but the lower garment is a mini-skirt and its upper edge is secured by three bands fastened in front by a medallion-like clasp. She adorns three necklaces in which the middle one is the smallest of the three which has a set of four cylindrical pendants. The largest necklace is hanging on the bare chest just between the bare conical breasts.

This also has a conical pendant in the middle. The eyes are shown by two round flat pellets of clay and her nose is pinched. The mouth is made of arrow of strips of clay and grooved along the middle to represent the lips. 'The figure is hand-modelled and the workmanship is rough and crude but the strips are marked in a great sophisticated manner. The jewellery, dress and other minor anatomical parts are fixed with pellets and strips of clay by the applique method. The right arm is missing but the left hangs stiffly at her side and the fingers are not marked in the hand. These female figurines are mother goddesses and are grouped as auspicious or fertility images and might have served some religious purpose. Marshall clarified these female figurines with elaborate headdress and jewellery as sacred images of mother goddess.

The female figurines are extremely common in most Harappan sites, which are situated on the Western part or the nucleus region, and was close to East Asia where the worship of mother goddess was in prominence. But it is interesting to note that the figurine of mother goddess is very few from the eastern region or the periphery region of Indian sites. A few archaic crude female figurines were reported from Lothal, Dholavira, Rakhigarhi, Dhalewan and Banawali-all Harappan sites located in India. The elaborate type female figurines were made by professional artists. These female figurines represent the great mother goddess or the Lady of Heaven which was considered a special patroness of women. Its images were also found from the sites of Mesopotamia and Egypt and also in the Eastern Mediterranean regions of West Asia. This Harappan female figurine indicates its possible Mesopotamian origin and it was added to the National Museum collection in 1948 as a permanent loan from the Archaeological Survey of India.

This figurine also resembles another headless tall standing female figurine from Mohenjo-daro, now in the collection of National Museum of Karachi (Acc. No. N.N.K. 52. 1874). The height of the Karachi figure is 21 cm. and when it was complete its total height was probably around 30 cm. The pannier vessels-like headdress were also noticed in a few other female figurines from Mohenjo-daro now housed in the Karachi Museum. This figure was declared by experts as of outstanding importance. The stone sculptures of the Mature Harappan period rarely represent artistic achievements but such big images are very few. The female mother goddess provides a much broader base for understanding the Harappan civilization.

6. Pot bellied mother goddess
Circa 2700 B.C., Harappa
Terracotta Size 9.6´7.2´5.9 cms
Acc No. H P 130121/386
National Museum, New Delhi
(D. P. Sharma: 2002)

It is a rough crude, wheel-made, cream colours the potbelly mother goddess, which was acquired through the excavation from Mohenjodaro. The two hands and a baby and part of a necklace are missing; and the figurine is blurred out but some impressions indicate the possible presence of a baby.

The face and the headdress are interesting. It has a curved beak-like nose with a well-rounded lower lip. The ears resemble like a shell. The bare breasts are hemispherical and noticeably apart from each other. The abdomen is flat and the navel is indicated by a hole. The fingers are not shown and its elbow joints are thin.

It has a close fitting plain flat twin collars around. The headdress is remarkable. It covers the fore head as well as the crown. The interesting aspects are the four sun flowers attached to it along the periphery.

Two cup-shaped lamps on either side of the head indicate that the figurine could be a wick-type lamp stand.

The figure was made by pinching and pressing the clay. The nose was made by pressing a lump of wet clay. The eyes have been made by sticking pellets in the hollows.

This figurine resembles another terracotta figurine found at Harappa (Acc. No. 1603) now in Pakistan. The presence of babies makes the figure more attractive. She is adorned with a necklace of double strings with a circular pendant hanging down between the round bare breasts. Ear ornaments, eyes and breasts were prepared by round pellets.

This also resembles in art style a few other potbelly figures, one from Harappa, (Acc. No. 213/230) a few others from Mohenjo-daro and two from Banawali. The female figures from all these sites have bulbous body. The nose is pinched and thick.

The terracotta mother goddess figures of a penguin shape (Arctic bird) was also reported from Lothal, which confirms that the Harappan artists were aware of birds of the Arctic region. Round bellied hollow figurines of mother goddess were made by wheel. The body of this female figurines is roundish. Similar round-bodied figurines are also found at Harappa, Nausharo, Mohenjo-daro, Banawali, and Chanhudaro.

7. Short potbellied mother goddess (Fig. 95)
   Mohenjo-daro, C 2700-2100 B.C.
   Terracotta, Size 6 × 9 ′ 8.5 ′ 4 cm.
   Acc No. D.K. 5797/334 N.N. 27-78, 30-78
   National Museum, New Delhi
   (D.P. Sharma: 2002)

The short potbellied standing mother goddess from Mohenjo-daro was discovered through excavations from the D.K. area at the level of 14.4 feet below the surface. The

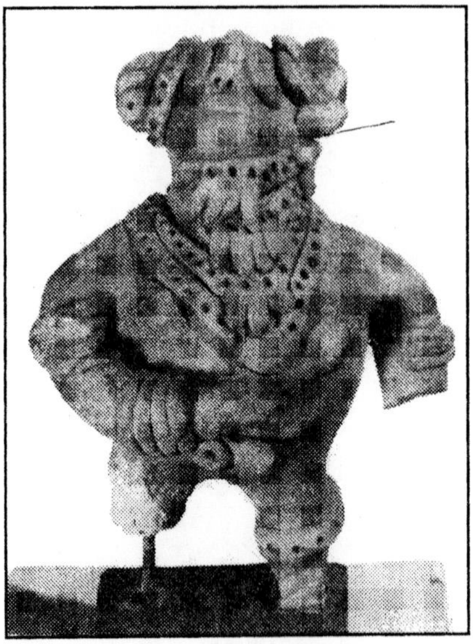

Fig. 95 : Potbellied short mother goddess C. 2700 B.C. Mohenjodaro, Terracotta, Neg No. 27-78, National Museum New Delhi Collection.

lower part of the left leg and right arm are missing. The figurine is completely hand-modelled and painted in red colour. The most noteworthy feature of this figurine is its elaborate jewellery. The figure is overloaded with necklaces consisting of heavy, beaded bands around the neck and cylindrical drop-like pendants which commonly hang from it. Such elaborate jewellery can be seen only in a few terracottas. The armlets and bracelets of spiral design are also represented here. The jewellery is fixed by the applique method of pellets and strips. The incised holes-type decoration marked on the necklace is interesting. Her fan-shaped headdress is broken. Although the short body structure is heavy and overloaded with jewellery, its overall charm remains eye-catching. The figurine is nude and has a pinched face. The bare round breasts and eyes were made of pellets and fixed by the applique method. The above figurine can also be in the mother goddess category because it has elaborate decoration.

During the Mature Harappan period a large number of terracotta female figurines (mother goddess) were reported from various sites. The antiquity of terracotta female mother goddess / fertility cult can be traced back up to 7th millennium B.C. and the earliest figurine of clay was modelled by the artist of Mehrgarh in northern Baluchistan, (Pakistan). The artist could see in the cult of the motherhood the inherent power to procreate which was the base for human development. The potbelly suggests that this is the deity of the fertility cult.

8. Seated female figurine
   Circa 2700 B.C., Harappa
   Terracotta Ht. 11.7 cms.
   Acc.No. 557/373 Neg No. R. 2608
   National Museum, New Delhi
   (D.P. Sharma: 2002)

Another crude, hand-modeled, cream-coloured female figurine was acquired through the excavation at Harappa. She is probably seated on some object, which is missing. The lower portion below the knee and its two arms are missing. The row of banded hairstyle is peculiar and appears like a plait which reminds us of the present day hair style of Indian women. The figurine is adorned with a close-fitted necklace of four beads and also with a long necklace of three strings which closes in a triangular clasp of unusual shape. The typical hair style of this figurine resembles that of another female terracotta from Chanhudaro. The figure is semi-nude with a prominent navel indicated by a hole. It does not have a navel ridge. The hips are well rounded and large. The chin is quite broad. The neck is rather thick and short, concealed by a plain, flat collar-band with suspended pendants of triangular shape.

The headdress resembles an open fan. It fits closely and covers the whole of the forehead extending up to the eye brows. The nostrils are prominent. The body is bare save for a narrow hand covering the private parts. The hair is plaited in a number of cylindrical coils and freely suspended and held in position by the opening of the head gear.

The hairstyle of this figurine looks almost similar to another terracotta figurine discovered by Marshall at Mohenjo-daro. The majority of the figurines available are in the standing posture and very few are in the sitting posture. A few important, seated figurines are shown kneading dough or seated on a three-legged stool with their hands holding the stool. The earlier theory that the representation of the stool in Indian art was first noticed during the Kusana period is not correct as is proved by the finds described above.

Animal Figurines

The terracotta animal figurines were found in abundance from the Harappan sites in the north west part of South Asia. The bull, a figure in various types, is the most dominant animal representing the Harappan civilization whereas other animal figurines are limited in number.

The terracotta bull figurines have been reported from almost all Early and Mature Harappan excavated sites like Nindowari, Harappa, Kotdiji, Chanhudaro, Amri, Rakhigarhi, Lothal, Padri, Kalibangan, Kuntasi, Banawali, Dholavira, Kulli-Mehi, Jalilpur, Nausharo, Allahdino, Mehrgarh, Sotkakoh, Sutkagendor, Bala-Kot, Gumla, Sarai-Khola, Rehman-Dehri, Mudigigak IV, Shortagai, Periogundai, Dabarkot, Jandhanawala, Daam Sadaat, Lurewala, Ganweriwala, Hisan-Dheri, Spiano Daam Gundai, Kunal, Rangpur, Anjira, Quetta, Dhalewan, Siswal, Bara, Hulas, Karchat, Ghazi-Shah, Lohemiodaro, Dabar-Kot, Kile-Gul-Mohammad, Hathnala, Mitathal Ropar, Surkotada, Niaibuthi, Ali Murad, Surjakgal, Lewan, Ballu, Shahi-Tumb, Pandi-Wohi, Nal, Ghaligahai, Nundara,

Siah Damb, Jhukar, Bet Dwarika, etc. Bull figurines are mostly hand-made but each one from Surkotada, Kalibangan and Harappa are mould-and-wheel made. These bull figurines are of five varieties as indicated below:

(i) Humped Bull or Brahmani Bull (Bos Indicus)
(ii) Bull without hump (Bos-Taurus)
(iii) Short-horned bull with hump
(iv) Humped bull with long horn
(v) Bull head or Anthropomorphic Taurine shape (*NANDIPADA*)

The Harappan period bulls are mostly unpainted but a few figurines from Amri, Kalibangan, and Surkotada are painted. These are mostly elongated.

At Kalibangan one painted bull figurine without a hump was found which is now exhibited in the National Museum, New Delhi. The bull figurines of Harappan style are shown with a stout or muscular body. The eyes, mouth and other details of the face are indicated by a hole and incision lines. At Harappa and Chanhudaro the eyes of the bull in a few figurines are separately made in disc shape and stuck to the face, but in the bull figurines from Kotdiji and a few other sites the eyes are shown by the incision technique. In the majority of these figurines the nostril is indicated just above the mouth.

The art style of the short-horned bull figurines from the Harappan sites is characteristically modelled. The tails in these are marked by incision lines. A few bull figurines wear garlands round their necks. The bull head of the long horn type or Anthropomorphic type of Taurine shapes were also seen on the pottery from Mohenjo-daro, Kunal and the Cemetry of Harappa. A large number of bull figurines along with clay pots were recently discovered from Rakhigarhi. It is likely that Rakhigarhi in Haryana was a big Harappan Agriculture Animal husbandry centre and these were cities supplying surplus food and milk product to the other Harappan cities. A few rare Bull figurines from the Harappan sites in the National Museum collection are described in the second part of this chapter.

The second popular domestic animal of the Harappan civilization is the buffalo (Babulus) and a few rare figurines in the National Museum collection are described in the third part of this chapter. The wild water buffalo forms are also present in the Early and Mature Harappan sites.

The elephant is another popular domestic animal as terracotta figurines of this animal have been reported from Harappa, Mohenjo-daro, Nausharo and Chanhudaro. These figurines are devoid of any decoration. However, the National Museum, India does not have any terracotta figurines of this animal. The Harappan Elephant (Elephas maximus) in terracotta was reported from Nausharo III period (mature Harappan). This is a part of a three-headed composite beast. The elephant figurines are hollow and a few well preserved pieces found at Mohenjo-daro and Nausharo III period are now in Pakistan. The elephant figurines from Chanhudaro have short trunks and short legs. Its spiral ridge and the sloping hindquarters are well modelled. It is also painted all over the body with sloping horizontal lines in red colour, and a red ring round the trunk and vertical lines in the front are comparable to the elephants dressed for the ceremonial procession in our times. Elephant figures were also found on steatite seals and copper tablets. The elephant was a symbol of trade and were exported for its ivory to West Asian countries. Elephant tusks and other elephant ivory items have been discovered at warehouses in Lothal and other sites.

A large number of figurines of dogs were reported from the Harappan sites. The dog was domesticated in south Asia from the early Neolithic period and this has been confirmed after the discovery of a dog burial from the Neolithic period sites at Burzhom in Kashmir. The antiquity of domestication of the wild dog goes even up to the Mesolithic or epipalaeolithic period (c 10000 B.C.) in European, Middle Eastern and western Asian sites. The earliest terracotta dog in South Asia was discovered from Mehrgarh from the early Chalcolithic level, which has been dated around C 4500 B.C. Terracotta figures of the dog were also reported at Harappan levels from Gumla II, Sariakbla, Kulli-Mehi, Harappa, Mohenjo-daro, Rakhigarhi, Chanhudaro, Lothal, Kalibangan, Dholavira & Nausharo, all Harappan sites in south Asia. The dog figurine of Mohenjo-daro bears close resemblance with another dog figurine from Lothal and Banawali. There is a controversy about the existence of the horse (Equus cabulus) during the Mature Harappan period. Earlier scholars were of the opinion that horses were brought in by the Aryans who were destroyers of the Harappan civilization. The Terracotta figurine of the horse comes from the Harappan sites like Mohenjo-daro, Banawali, Nausharo, Rakhigarhi, Lothal, Piraq, Rangpur, and Surkotada. Mackay has identified one terracotta horse from Mohenjo-daro, which is now exhibited in the National Museum at New Delhi. This figurine has a long back and a thick neck, a broken tail, short erect ears and patches all over the body. The skeleton remains of the bones of the horse have been discovered from Lothal, Surkotada, Padri, Rana-Gundai, Harappa, Kalibangan and Periano-Gundai. The remains of these figurines' bones suggest the presence of the horse Linn (Equus cabulus) during the Mature Harappan period. The theory about a Aryan invasion on the Harappans is now out-dated. Now scholars believe that the first Aryans were indigenous people and they did not come from outside India. D.P. Sharma also believes that the Dravidian and first Aryan were native people. The Aryan and proto-Dravidian people were very well present in the Mature Harappan population. The earliest Aryan or the early Vedic people existed in South Asia since the Early Harappan period 3500-2700 B.C.

The monkey is also represented as terracotta figures of this animal were found at Mohenjo-daro, Harappa, Rakhigarhi, Kalibangan, Chanhudaro, Periano-Gundai, and Lothal. The monkey figurine of Lothal resembles the African gorilla. They modelled these figurines in two styles. Firstly, those with their skin treated in a naturalistic manner; secondly, with skin indicated by incision lines. The world famous toy of a climbing monkey from Harappa, now in the National Museum, New Delhi, is very attractive. The hair of the body, the spinal cord, the back portion, etc., are indicated by incision lines. This figure is beautifully modelled with the end of the tail turned down very naturalistically. The jumping posture of this monkey from Harappa and Mohenjo-daro are of special attraction. Miniature faience and paste models of monkeys from Mohenjo-daro are of great artistic value.

The figurines of Ram modelled in clay are reported from Harappa, Chanhudaro, Mohenjo-daro, Nal, Mehi, Lothal, Banawali, Rakhigarhi, Bhagwanpura, Hulas and Alamgirpur. Wheeled carts driven by the Ram from Bhagwanpura and Alamgirpur were made for the amusement of children. Vibha Tripathi classified Ram figurines in three groups as follows:

(i) In which wrinkled skin is represented by the incision lines,

(ii) In which the wrinkle of the skin is represented by the incised, small parabolic line,

(iii) In which the wrinkle of the skin is indicated by tiny holes.

A few heads of the Ram are very attractive. The Ram figures from Lothal are closer to those of Harappa, Mohenjodaro, Rakhigarhi and Banawali.

The Rhinoceros terracotta figurines were discovered from Harappa, Nausharo, Mohenjo-daro, Chanhudaro, Lothal, Kalibangan, Banawali, etc. The wrinkled hide of this animal was marked by incision lines and fitted patches over the shoulders. The snout of this animal is attractively marked and the eyes are shown by round pellets with incised holes to denote the pupils. Some of these have collar-like bands around the necks, but these are more likely to be represented on a fold of skin on the neck rather than on the collar. The body of the Rhinoceros is short which gives the impression that the artist who modelled this animal was not well acquainted with the anatomy of the animal.

Other animals in terracotta are the hare, snakes, pigs, squirrels, buffaloes, antelopes, etc. The buffalo was the second largest animal after the bull figurines. At the Harappan sites the buffalo is shown as a bellied animal in a typical attitude with its head up.

The following are a few rare animal figurines in the National Museum of India, New Delhi Collection:

9. Horse, (Equus caballus)
   Circa 2300 B.C., Mohenjo-daro
   Terracotta (Fig. 96)
   Ht. 7.5 cms Neg No. T-203, R 1667
   Acc No. D. K. 4732/237,
   National Museum, New Delhi
   (D. P. Sharma: 2002)

This is a hand-made figurine of the horse. It has a white slip and its legs and tail portion are missing. Prof B.B. Lal recently observed on the basis of the Art style and

Fig. 96 : Horse (Equus caballus) C. 2300 B.C. Mohenjodaro, Terracotta, Neg No. T-703, R1667, Acc No. D.K. 4732/287 National Museum, New Delhi

anatomical details that this seemed to be a figurine of the horse (Equus caballus). Very few terracotta figurines of the horse have been reported from the Mature Harappan sites. The horse is rare and it seems the horse reached Harappan sites towards the end of the Mature Harappan period when the Vedic Aryans came in contact with the late Mature Harappan people. On the basis of the discovery of the skeleton and bones of the domestic variety of the horse from the late-Mature Harappan deposit of Surkotada, it may be concluded that the late Mature Harappan people were domesticating the horse. However, scholars are of the opinion that only a few specimens from the Harappan sites are not sufficient to confirm this fact. The Harappan were domesticating the horse. Terracotta figurines of the horse were also reported from the late Nausharo and Banawali Mature Harappan deposits of Lothal, Rangpur.

The horse was known to the Mature Harappans and a few clay figurines and bone resembling the domesticated horse came from different Harappan sites viz. Mohenjo-daro, Rakhigarhi, Lothal, Rangpur, Nausharo, Padri and Pirak (Last site is late Harappan) (Fig. 97). Mackay identified the above figurines of Mohenjo-daro as the horse. The horse from Mohenjo-daro has a long back, a thin neck, a broken tail, short erect ears and patches all over the body. Marshall and Mackay have identified this as the horse. Rao reported horse terracotta figurines from Lothal and Rangpur. A. Stein reported fragments of the horse from the Indus area in which the curvature of the neck looks like that of the horse. Skeleton (bone) remains of the domestic variety of the horse have been reported from the Rana-Gundai, Kalibangan and Surkotada. The above archaeological finds confirms the presence of the horse in the Harappan times, which reached there along with the Early Aryans or the Aryans of the copper hoard period. R. Meadow & Ajita Patel are of the opinion that this is an ass (Equus Heminonus) and not the horse (Equus caballus). D.P. Sharma and Madhuri Sharma are of the view that this is a horse (Equus caballus). R.S. Sharma concluded that the horse came on the Harappan scene during the end of its mature phase. A terracotta figurine of the horse was discovered from Piraq (2000 B.C.)

Fig. 97 : Horse from Banawali

10. Unicorn (Fig. 98)
Circa 2700 B.C., Chanhudaro
Terracotta, Size 4.8 ´5.2 cm
Acc. No. CH-43/305 Neg No. R 1568
National Museum, New Delhi
(D. P. Sharma: 2002)

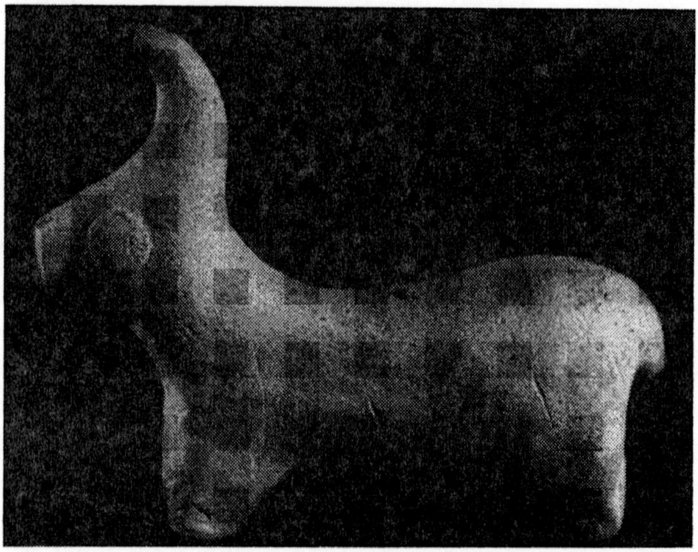

Fig. 98 : Unicorn figurine. Circa 2700 B.C. Terracotta Chanhudaro. Acc No. CH-43/305, N.M. R1568, National Museum, New Delhi Collection

Another interesting terracotta figurine in the collection is of a unicorn (mythical animal). The figurine is rough hand modelled and has a coating of red slip. The mythical animal has one horn, a mouth and two eyes. The tail portion of this figure is missing and there are four slanting engraved strokes on the body. The pair of front and hind legs is shown jointly. The unicorn animal figurine which is also depicted on about twelve per cent seals and pottery of the Harappan seems to be a mythical animal and this can also be associated with some ritual which was very popular with the Harappans. The body of the unicorn appears like that of a Rhinoceros and the head resembles that of the Tibetan deer. Some archaeologists have named this as Anthronop. The face of this animal is round and the body is comparatively bigger in size and the pairs of legs are thick and appear like those of a bovine-Animal. The tail, neck, ears are comparatively smaller in size. The figures of the unicorn animal were also noted in groups of prehistoric paintings in Lauscax cave, in Europe and these paintings are dated around C. 10000 B.C. This animal figure appears like a combination of a bull and a horse. The terracotta animal figures of the unicorn, dated 700 A.D., were also reported from Tibet which is now in the central Asian art collection of the National Museum, New Delhi. The terracotta figurines of the Tibetan deer were also found from Mohenjo-daro, which partly resembles the unicorn figure. The pair of bulls in bronze figure from Daimabad chariot shows some similarity with that of the unicorn or horse. This figure partly resembles the terracotta Rhino figure of Kalibangan. The unicorn figure is also on the polychrome pots of Nal dated C 3300 B.C, which is on display in the Harappa gallery of the National Museum, New Delhi. On the basis of the above-mentioned references it may be said that the unicorn was a mythical animal and was found from c 10000 B.C. to 700 A.D. Terracotta figurines of unicorn were also reported from Dholavira and three others were discovered at Chanhudaro.

Bird Terracotta Figurines

Bird terracotta figurines were reported in large numbers from various sites of the Harappan civilization. Birds like hen, peacock, etc., were hand-modelled with great care. Some figurines have holes on the underside for separate insertion of feet or pedestals. The wings of these birds are shown in relief and the feathers by incision lines. A few birds in terracotta identified are a parrot, a flying-sparrow, a seated hen, a pigeon, a cock, a duck, a goose, etc. Bone fragments of these birds were also reported from the mature Harappan sites. Some birds with holes were used as toy whistles. Rare bird figurines in the collection of the National Museum, New Delhi, are as follows:

11. Man holding a duck (Fig. 99)
 Circa 2700-2000 B.C., Harappa
 Terracotta Acc. No. 4925/373
 Size 7´2.5´2.7 cm, Neg No. 4356-77
 National Museum, New Delhi
 (D.P. Sharma: 2002)

What many consider as a common place occurrence sometimes catches the eye of an artist and spurs him on to his best creativity, and the result is a great work of art. The example of a terracotta figurine of a man holding a struggling duck firmly to his chest is one such. What attracted the artist's attention was the strong resolve of the man and the bird-the former to hold the captured duck in bondage and the latter to struggle for freedom. Bondage and freedom-the never ceasing themes-hold a peculiar fascination for those who have suffered bondage and realized the joys of freedom.

Fig. 99 : Man holding a duck, Harappa, 2700 B.C. National Museum New Delhi Collection.

The artist chose a perfect medium to immortalize this theme–the common clay. Perhaps he made the figure deliberately crude to obscure his idea and escape the arm of the law in a rigid society, which the Harappan society probably was, as indicated by the severity of standardization then prevalent.

The nudity of the man, his missing legs, the pinched pellets of his thin eyes all these do not detract the viewer from the main focus of the struggle between the man and the bird.

It is indeed amazing to note that such great artists lived and worked so long ago. This piece is a lasting tribute to the art of the mature Harappan and their boldness of sport and imagination.

6

Seals, Sealings and Copper Tables

The seals bear decorative motifs with or without inscriptions, cut in intaglio in the negative form. When a seal was impressed on wet clay or plasticine or any plastic material, it produced the same pattern in relief in the positive. Hence, the seal impression on any plastic material is called sealing (Fig. 100).

Fig. 100 : Terracotta sealing from Dholavira C. 2600-2000 B.C. A.S.I. New Delhi Collection.

Most of the rectangular copper tablets, both the embossed and engraved ones, may have been used as tokens. So far around 142 copper tablets have been reported mostly from Mohenjo-daro and three from Indian sites. Engravings on these tablets are not so deep as to warrant their use for stamping purposes. A few zinc or silver and copper seals are cut in the negative and these were used for making seal impressions.

The earliest stamp seals, datable to (Fig. 101) 5516 B.C., were discovered from Hussuna, a site in ancient Mesopotamia. Around 3500 B.C. stamp seals were replaced in Mesopotamia by the cylindrical seals as these had the advantage of sealing a larger area of wet clay. The square seal with round corners datable to circa 3300 B.C. was discovered through excavations at Rehman-Dehri in Pakistan (Fig. 102). The round seals were in use in Anatolia, Behrain and Iran during third millennium B.C.

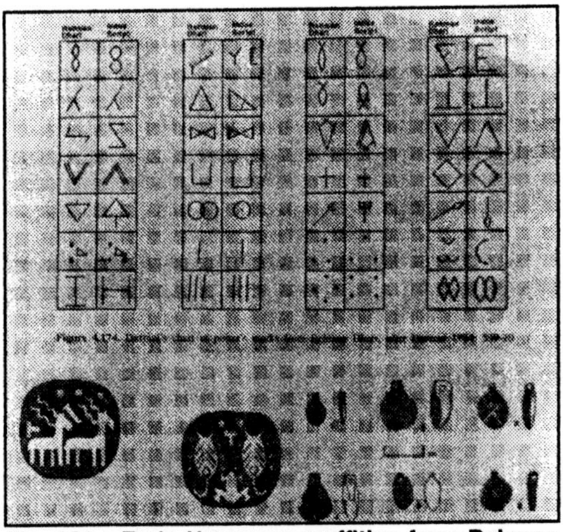

Fig. 101 : Early Harappan graffitles from Rehman Dehri and other early Harappan sites (3000-2000 B.C.) Neg 2/23-2000 (N.M.) Photograph after Asthana; 1980.

Fig. 102 : Square with round corner seal from Rehmandehri (Pakistan) C. 3000-2800 B.C. (Pre Harappan Period)

One of the most outstanding finds dated circa 3200 B.C. (early Harappan period) from Mehrgarh is a somewhat rectangular terracotta seal. Similar types of stamp of early Harappan seals were also reported from Kunal, Nagawada, Mundigak and a few other sites in South Asia. The Early Harappan culture also produced a few rectangular steatite seals of Indus style, without inscription with geometric motifs like a concentric triangle etc. So far seven seals of the Harappan style have been reported from Kunal in Hissar district of Haryana, and three from Sherikhan Tarakai in Pakistan-all ascribed between circa 3000-2800 B.C.

These mature Harappan seals with the negative engraving of animal figures along with inscriptions in Harappan script are datable to the mid 3rd millennium B.C. The seals with inscriptions and without animal figures are dated mostly to the late Harappan period (circa 2000-1500 B.C.). A few Harappan graffiti marks continued even up to circa 1500-1000 B.C. the Double knot sign typical of the Harappan script was recently reported in the Megalithic monument of South India.

Shapes and sizes

These seals are mostly square or rectangular in shape with a perforated hemispherical boss on their back to facilitate their handling. Some unusual shapes are cylindrical, crescent, button like, cubical, hexagonal, round, rhomboid, triangular, prism, tetrahedrons, lance shape, heart shape, shield leaf, fish-shape and spherical. The rectangular seals differ in shape from the seals of West Asia, i.e. Mesopotamia and Egypt, which are cylindrical. A few round seals and sealings reported from Rakhigarhi, Lothal, Mohenjo-daro and cylindrical seals from Mohenjo-daro, Sibiri and Kalibangan are of West Asia origin (Fig. 103b). The length of the Harappan seals is between

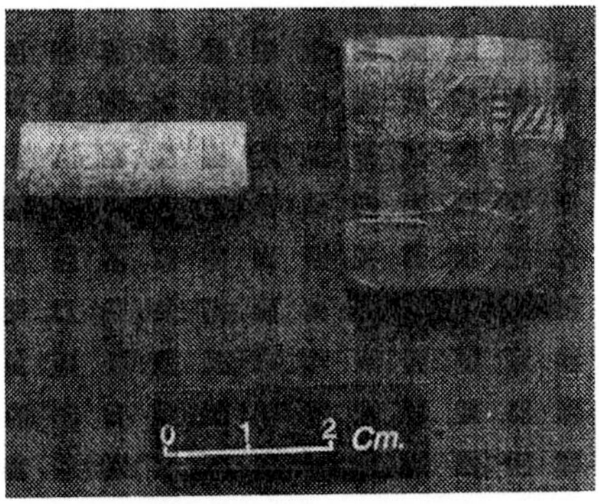

Fig. 103 : Cylyndrical Seal Faience, and its impression, C.2500 B.C., Rakhigarhi, A.S.I. Collection, Photograph after Amrendra Nath : 2000

3/4" to 2" '/2'. So far, around 5516 seals, copper tablets, sealings and inscriptions have been reported from the various Harappan sites. The National Museum, New Delhi, has in its collection 167 seals, sealings and some 35 copper tablets from Mohenjo-daro and 55 seals as loan from A.S.I. which were discovered from Lothal, Kalibangan, Rakhigarhi, Banawali, Dholavira, Dhalewan and other sites.

Material and technique

These seals are mostly made of soft steatite (Chlorite) or french chalk of white, black, gray and dull yellow colour. Besides this, they also used powder steatite, faience, and silver, zink, copper, bone, ivory, glazed terracotta, limestone and marble but rarely. The unfinished seals discovered at Chanhudaro show that the different stages of the manufacturing process are on display. Some terracotta, faience and paste seals were made by mould and their inscription was inscribed afterward.

These seals and sealings insignia of ownership and the main purpose of these inscribed visuals were to authenticate documents such as receipts, contracts, deeds, etc. Seals were also used for administrative purposes and various stamping activities primarily for the utilitarian function as a means of identification.

The following are some of the rare seals in the collection of the National Museum of India:

1. *Pasupati or Proto-Siva Seal*
   Mature Harappan (circa 2700-2000 B.C.), Mohenjo-daro Steatite,
   Size: (1-6/16 ′ 1-6/16 ′ 1/4)"
   N. No. 1981-66, 1263-76
   Acc. No. DK 5175/143
   National Museum, New Delhi
   (D. P. Sharma: 2001)

This unique square steatite seal depicts the figure of a god seated in yogic posture on his heels with knees apart. He has three faces and is surrounded by animals. The Crowning head has two horns. His hands, fully covered with bangles, rest on the knees. On top there is an inscription. Three seals of this type were reported from Mohenjo-daro. Siva is called Pasupati or lord of animals. The Pasupati figure is also painted on a big jar from Padri and also on the pots excavated from Kotdiji, Burzhom and Kunal, which are dated up to circa 2800 B.C. to 2600 B.C. (Fig. 104)

Fig. 103 : Storage jar depicting *Pasupati*, C.2800 B.C. pottery, Padri Deccan College Poona Collection.

2. *Unicorn before an Incense Burner*
   Mature Harappan (circa 2700-2000 B.C.) Harappa
   Steatite, Square
   Size 1.55 ´ 1.55" Acc. No. 11942/2
   N. No. 4368-76, 337-77, 1623-63, 1624-63
   National Museum, New Delhi
   (D. P. Sharma: 2001)

The most frequently represented animal on the seals is unicorn. The unicorn is shown as standing in front of an incense burner, a joint pot consisting of two vessels joined by a staff. Unicorns of terracotta have been reported from Chanhudaro, Dholavira and the representation of this animal continued till the early historic period in Central Asian art. The incense burner is also embossed on two gold fillets, which were discovered from the jewellery hoard discovered from Mohenjo-daro.

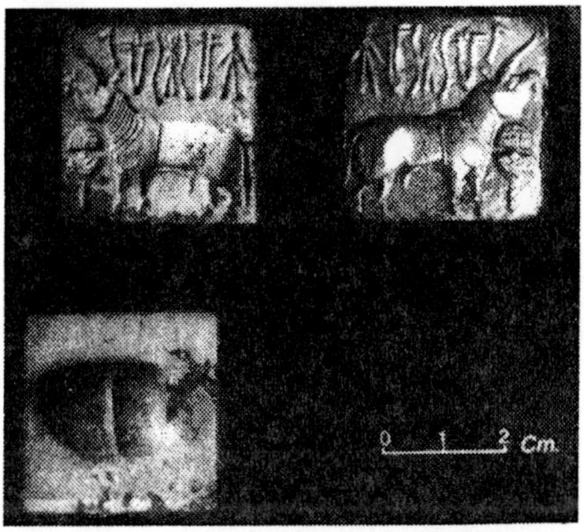

Fig. 105 : Unicorn seals from Rakhigarhi. Photograph after A. nath : 1999. Neg No. 15-2000 (N.N) A.S.I. New Delhi Collection.

3. *Seal showing a Man between two Tigers*
   Mature Harappan (circa 2700-2000 B.C.), Mohenjo-daro Steatite, (Fig. 106)
   Size: (1-1/4 ´ 1-1/4 ´ 5/6)"
   N. No. 2029-2030-66, 1262-76
   Acc. No. DK 12596/145
   National Museum, New Delhi
   (D.P. Sharma: 2001)

This is a brown square steatite seal with a perforated boss on the reverse, showing a man holding two tigers by his hands. It shows a male figure standing between two standing roaring tigers. Another seal of this type from Mohenjo-daro is in Pakistan collection.

Fig. 106 : Seal showing man between tigers. 2500 B.C. Mohenjodaro. Acc No. D.K. 12596/145, Neg No. 2030-66. National Museum New Delhi

4. *A Pipal Tree and Unicorn Heads*
(circa 2700-2000 B.C.),
Mohenjo-daro Steatite, (Fig. 107)
Size: 1-5/16 ´ 1-5/16" Acc. No. B 63/74
N. No. 83-61, 1255-76
National Museum, New Delhi
(D.P. Sharma: 2001)

A square steatite seal from Mohenjo-daro shows the '*pipal*' (Ficus religiosus), flanked by the curving and serrated neck of the unicorns which emerge from a petalled boss affixed to the centre of the trunk. The lower portions are inscribed upon. In India the *pipal* is worshiped as (*purusha*) the male deity and the triangular symbols below it as the female deity (*Prakrit*). This feature is noticed in many ancient and modern temples where the *pipal* and triangular signs are seen together.

5. *Seal depicting Swastika*

Mature Harappan (circa 2700-2000 B.C.), Harappa,

Faience, (rare) Size: 1.2 ´ 1 .2"

N. No. 1128-76, Acc. No. 12890/21

National Museum, New Delhi

(D.P. Sharma: 2001)

Fig. 107 : Pipal and Unicorn Seal

The *Swastika* motif is frequently found on the Harappan seals. The *Swastika* is also found in Crete, Babylonia, Egypt, Iran and other countries. This symbol was known in South Asia since Circa 3500 B.C. The earliest evidence is found on the ceramics from Mehrgarh and Shahi Tump in Baluchistan and Rakhigarhi-all belonging to the early Harappan period. The Harappan *Swastika* is mostly clockwise in direction but a few are anti-clock-wise, which confirms the existence of two major racial groups in Harappan population.

6. *Seal showing Humped Bull*

Mature Harappan (circa 2700-2000 B.C.), Mohenjo-daro Steatite, (Fig. 108)
Size: (1-5/15 ´ 1-5/16 ´ 5/16)"
N. No. 2035 To 36-66, 325-77, 84-61
Acc. No. HR 3087/105
National Museum, New Delhi
(D. P. Sharma: 2001)

This is a grey square steatite seal with a perforated boss on the reverse showing an engraved bull with long horns and heavy wrinkled develop facing left. It depicts the humped bull standing in profile. The lower right corner of the seal is broken. The seal, showing the humped bull, has been discovered from all the Harappan sites.

Besides these, there are a few more seals from Dholavira, Banawali, Lothal and Rakhigarhi which are on display in the National Museum, New Delhi.

Fig. 108 : Seal showing humped bull, Mohenjodaro. Neg. No. 5/26-200.

Script and Language

The term Harappan script includes the mature Harappan as well as the late Harappan script. It used pictures of animate and inanimate objects along with few linear signs resembling Roman-like characters.

The Harappan script is on the final way of decipherment for which attempts and researches are going on in this direction. One factor favours the identification of the Harappan language as Dravidian due to the presence of Brahui language as in the immediate vicinity of Harappa. The second language of Harappan Civilization was *Laukik* (popular) Sanskrit. The authors of the ochre - coloured ceramics and the copper hoards of western India were perhaps the early Aryan settlers in South Asian region and they inhabited in this region during circa 2800-1100 B.C. They were speaking *Laukik* Sanskrit language.

During the early and mature Harappan periods the people were speaking a bi-lingual language i.e. proto-

Dravidian Brahui and *Laukik Sanskrit*. Later on, around 2000 B.C. when Dravidian speaking people migrated from this area towards South India, *Laukik Sanskrit* became the first language. We do not have longer and bi-scriptal inscriptions of the Harappan script like those of the Rosetta stone and Takht-I-Bahai inscription of West Asia. Nearly 5516 short Harappan inscriptions have been reported. The preserved written texts are also very short and they have maximum 19 signs and pictures. A three-sided sealing has 27 signs, which is on display in National Museum, New Delhi.

A unique find is one inscribed double-headed Anthropomorphic form of Siva figurine of a terracotta reported from Kalibangan. This object has an inscription in proto-Brahmi script, which gives some clue about the Harappan script. The middle part of neck portion of this figurine has three engraved signs in Harappan script. First, one which is on the top appears like Sa i.e. Jar sign and second is of a circle with two parallel lines and third sign is like a taurine symbol or knot design or Brahmi *Maor* number four in Devanagari or English number eight (8).

This mould-made double-headed human head was discovered at Kalibangan. The taurine (*Nandipada*) symbol is on the forehead. The Art style of this is typical mature Harappan. Another male terracotta bust from Kalibangan also has some graffiti marks. These three signs on Siva head appear like proto-Brahmi or Archaic Brahmi and the inscription can be read as SIVAM. (शिवम्)

NANDIPADA OR TAURINE SYMBOL (SIVAM)

This inscription is in *proto-Brahmi* script and its language is *Laukik Sanskrit*. On the basis of the inscribed Siva figurine, the script of the Harappans has a close resemblance with *Proto-Brahmi*. One group of Harappan population was of Aryan race and they were speaking *Laukik Sanskrit* language. It has also been observed that the group of early Harappan people and ochre-coloured pottery were the earliest Aryan settlers in South Asia and their language was perhaps *Laukik Sanskrit*. Their culture was contemporary to the Harappan civilization. A signboard inscription from Dholavira of mature Harappan can throw more light on decipherment of the Harappan script and its model is on display in National Museum, New Delhi (Fig. 109). The 1500 B.C. old bi-scriptal inscription discovered by S. R. Rao at Bet Dwarika confirms that by this time the writing system was from left to right and a few proto Brahmi signs are very well present in this

Fig. 109

inscription. The use of the Harappan script continued even up to 1500 B.C. There are evidences of inscriptions from Alamgirpur and other Harappan sites of western Uttar Pradesh to prove this conjecture (Fig. 110). The Harappan

Fig. 110 : Late Harappan Pot inscription from Bet Dwarika, Neg No. 306-2001, N.I.O. Goa Collection.

script was carved, incised, chiseled, inlaid, painted, moulded and embossed mostly negative and rarely positive-(raised) on terracotta (clay), glazed pottery, shell, bone, ivory, sand stone, steatite, gypsum, copper, bronze, silver, zinc, gold and other material. We can conclude that the Harappan script was woven into fabrics and basketry, carved and inlaid in wood, inscribed on palm leaves and were painted on jars and the human body and other materials. The writing system of script was mostly written from right to left as in practice in the Semitic, Arabic, Hebrew, Aramaic and Kharosthi scripts of West and South Asia, 10 to 15 percent Harappan inscriptions were written from left to right as in the practice of *Brahmi* and *Sanku* scripts of South Asia. *Proto-Brahmi* script was written from right to left and after 1500 B.C. South Asians were writing early Brahmi script from left to right which continued during early historic period (6th. C.B.C. to 7th Century A.D.)

as well. There is a longer moulded and embossed-Harappan of a two-line inscription where the first line proceeds from right to left and the second line reads from left to right like the *Kharoshti* script. Alternating directions of the writing system was called Bostrophedon (both sides).

7

Jewellery

The earliest occurrence of copper beads (jewellery) goes back to 8th millennium B.C. from the sites of West Asia and the Middle East region of the Levant. In South Asia (India) the earliest date of bone-clay ornaments have been reported from Mahadaha and Mehrgarh and the C-14 date of these sites comes around circa 8000-7000 B.C (Fig. 111). Around circa 2700-2000 B.C., mature Harappan craftsmen became skilled bead-makers and during this period the drilling, perforation and chipping of beads was in practice by the hard drill-bits made of hard stone. Drill bits made of hard stone have been reported from Dholavira, Lothal, Chanhudaro, Harappa, Allahadino,

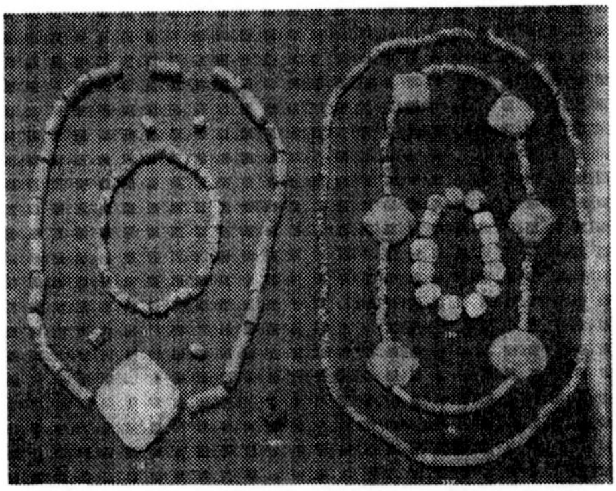

Fig. 111 : Shell, Terracotta and Lapis Lazuli necklaces beads, C.7000-4500 B.C. Mehrgarh, National Museum, Karachi Collection, Photograph after Kondo, 2001.

Nausharo and Mohenjo-daro-all these are mature Harappan sites.

In India the oldest gold items of jewellery i.e., cup-shaped beads were reported from Nagwada (Gujarat), Nindawari and Kunal (Haryana) and these are dated up to circa 3000 B.C. These jewellery items of the mature Harappan period are identical in the high technical skill of a metal-smith and its manufacturing method shows uniformity. For spring design the Harappan craftsmen were expert at making the thin wire of gold and silver and they also knew the repousse' technique over the jewellery items.

The Harappan gold jewellery items from the mature Harappan sites consist of various types like bracelets, necklaces, bangles, ear and head ornaments, ring, brooches, girdles, etc.

The mature Harappan gold items are of typical light colour, which is a natural alloy (Electrum) of gold and silver that has 96.3% gold and 3.7% silver. Gold and silver ornaments along with goldsmith workshop of bead making, gold smith's house and gold mould were also reported through excavation from Rohira (Punjab), India.

Two necklaces from Lothal, which are made of tiny gold beads and round silver beads are of great attraction. Rakhigarhi gold jewellery items consist of gold fillet and head ornaments, armlets and beads. Four silver bangles were also reported from Rakhigarhi.

Gold items from Dholavira are ear ornaments, beads, wire and miniature pin shaped object, which appears like a threading needle, and is identical in shape with two other needles discovered from Mohenjo-daro. Gold items from Mohenjo-daro, Rakhigarhi, and Dholavira are displayed in the National Museum, New Delhi. The catalogue data of a few rare Harappan jewellery items are as follows:

1. Necklace (Fig 112).
   2700 B.C., Mohenjo-daro
   Gold and stone, Dia-6 cm
   N. No. 239-91, Acc. No.49.244
   National Museum, New Delhi
   (D. P. Sharma: 2002)

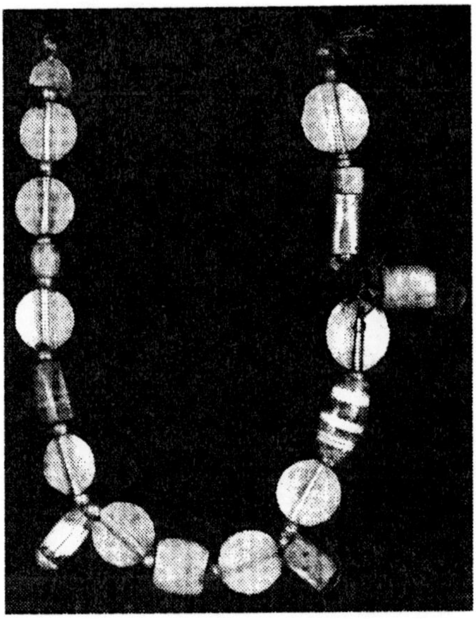

Fig. 112 : Necklace, Mohenjodaro, C.2700 B.C. gold and stone. Neg No. 239-91, Acc No. 49-244. National Museum New Delhi Collection.

This is part of a necklace composed of globular and disc-shaped gold beads, along with the beads of onyx, green-stone, turquoise and agate. There is a semi-circular terminal at one end of the necklace. The necklace consists of three stone beads, five green beads, nine disc-shaped beads of gold, one gold cylindrical bead and one gold terminal. Three stone beads have coping ends made of gold. The round disc-shaped beads are made of thin flat gold sheets inter-shaped with stone beads of onyx amazonite (Micro line), turquoise and banded agate. Some beads have gold finials and additional small spherical beads are also used as spacers.

This necklace portion is only half of the original ornament, which was divided between India and Pakistan in 1947. This was discovered from hoard No.3 H.R. area room 8, House VIII Block 2, through excavation at Mohenjo-daro. This necklace is identical with another semi-circular part of a necklace of Mohenjo-daro, which is housed in Mohenjo-daro Museum (M.M. 50.28/2/369). The Gold disc shaped beads of these two necklaces are identical with another similar gold necklace made of flat beads which of Mohenjo-daro now on display in the National Museum, New Delhi. The flat disc beads manufacturing technology is typical Harappan and a similar type of silver bead necklace of 2800 B.C. has been recently discovered from Kunal now in the collection of the state department of Archaeology, Haryana, Chandigarh. A disc shaped beads necklace of the mature Harappan period from Mandi is identical with the disc shaped beads necklaces from Mohenjo-daro.

2. Necklace of Gold and Stone Beads
   2700 B.C., Mohenjo-daro (Fig.113)
   Gold, Agate, Jade, Lizardite, etc.
   Wt. 719.2 grain with thread
   N. No. 4813-65 & 246-91, 238-91
   Acc. No. 49.244/105 (D. K. 1341)
   National Museum, New Delhi
   (D. P. Sharma: 2002)

This is the part of a long necklace consisting of double convex gold beads and barrel-shaped light green stone (Lizardite and Agate) beads and pendant. Four convex beads of gold separate the stone beads from each other. This has four stone barrel-shaped pendants in which two are agate and two, jade. The

Fig. 113 : Necklace, C.2700 B.C. Mohenjodaro, Gold and stone Agate, Jade, Lizardite Acc No. 49-244/105 (4010) Neg No. 4613-65, National Museum New Delhi

necklace consists of 4 jade beads, 4 pendants, 25 gold beads and 4 small steatite beads with a few tiny gold terminals. This necklace is exactly identical to the necklace adored by the bronze dancing girl from Mohenjo-daro which is now displayed in the Harappan gallery of the National Museum, New Delhi. This also shows similarity with the other part of the necklace from Mohenjo-daro, which is in Mohenjo-daro Museum and these two belong to one hoard No. 1, which was found in a silver vessel in D.K. area room No.2 of eastern end of Block IC section. Kenoyer identified the green stone material as Lizardite or grossularite. The length of these green stone beads is 2 cm. and diameter 1 cm. The shapes of the gold beads are double-convex hollow. The other part of this necklace is now in the collection of Pakistan Museum.

3. Needle (Fig. 114)
C 2700 B.C., Mohenjo-daro, Gold
Length: 6.4 cm, Wt. with thread 119.6 grain
N. No. 4714-65 & 245-91
Acc. No. 49.244-24 (62044)
National Museum, New Delhi
(D. P. Sharma: 2002)

This is a hollow cylindrical gold needle, which has a cylindrical point. This pin type object was used for spraying *sindur* or other powder or liquid during ceremony. An exactly identical gold needle from Mohenjo-daro is on display in the gallery of National Museum, Karachi. A miniature identical shape made of one gold and another of Faience were recently reported from Dholavira. These items are on

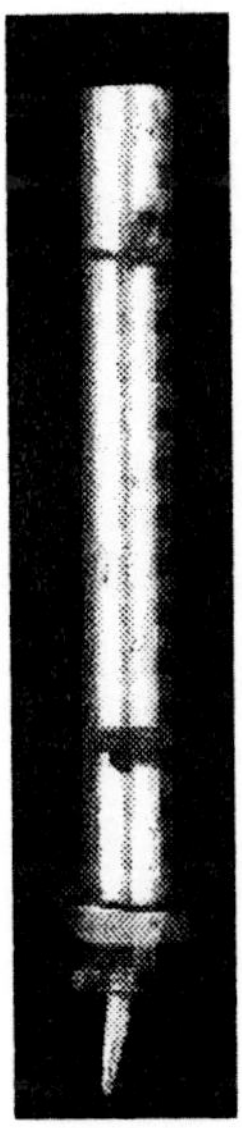

Fig. 114 : Needle of goldsmith, C. 2700 B.C. Mohenjodaro, Gold. Acc No. 49-244-24 (62044) Neg No. 245-91. National Museum, New Delhi Collection.

display in the Harappan gallery of National Museum, New Delhi. D.P. Sharma is of the view that these might have been used by the Harappan women for the pinching of face and also for decoration of the head. The exact purpose of this object is still unknown. Identically shaped copper, shell, and faience needle with eyehole were reported from Dholavira and other Harappan sites. Madhuri Sharma and Anamika Pathak are of the opinion that these needles of gold-two-from Mohenjo-daro and a miniature one from Dholavira-must have been used by the Harappan for threading golden wire. Copper, faience, shell and ivory holed needles must have been used by Harappan weavers.

4. Bead Choker necklace with six rows of gold beads
   2700 B.C., Mohenjo-daro
   Gold (Electrum) (Fig. 115)
   L. 9.6 cm, K.26
   Gold Bead 3cm L, Dia.27cm
   N. No. 243-91 4814-65
   Acc. No.49.244/23 (E.11)
   National Museum, New Delhi
   (D.P. Sharma: 2002)

Fig. 115 : Bead choker necklace (part) with six rows of beads, C.2700 B.C. Mohenjo-daro Gold (Electrum), Acc No. 49-244/23 (E11) Neg No. 4814-65. National Museum, New Delhi Collection.

This is part of a choker or tight necklace made of one hundred forty eight (148) tiny beads of gold, four spacers, and one terminal end of crescent shape. The round gold beads are arranged in six rows with divider bars and a half-moon shaped terminal, both made of gold. This is half the portion of the necklace, which was divided between India and Pakistan in 1947. This choker was discovered through excavation from hoard No.3 of H.R. area Room No. 8, House VII, Block 2, section B of Mohenjo-daro mound. The other half portion of this necklace is now on display in the Mohenjo-daro Museum (M.M. 1383.50.28)

5. Conical Head ornament
 2700 B.C.,Mohenjo-daro
 Gold (Fig. 116) & silver
 Ht: 3.5 cm, Dia 6.2, L 1.25 cm
 Wt. 122.5 grain, Acc. No. 49.2543
 N. No. 275-91 & 261-91, 259-91
 National Museum, New Delhi
 (D. P. Sharma: 2002)

This is a conical head ornament of gold with double rim at base. It has a silver hook near the apex, which was meant for a attachment. These items are hollow and made of thin gold sheets. A similar conical head-ornament is found on the forehead of a few female terracotta figurines discovered from Harappa, Mohenjo-daro and Nausharo. The married women of Nagaur area of Rajasthan still use a

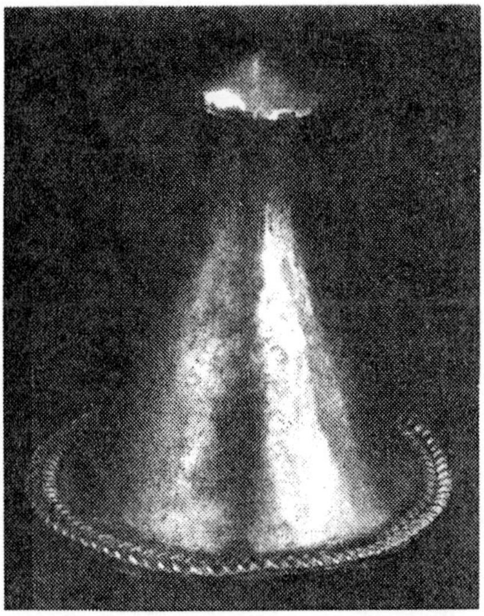

Fig. 116 : Conical Head ornament C.2700 B.C. Mohenjodaro. Gold and silver. Neg No. 259-91, Acc No. 49-2543 (49-244/10). National Museum, New Delhi Collection.

similar head ornament, which reminds us of the continuous tradition of the Harappan Civilization. An identical type of gold head ornaments was also reported from Mohenjo-daro and Allahdino, both Harappan sites. The head ornament, which is under discussion, was discovered from Trench IV mound F of Mohenjo-daro. A round shaped *Tika* very well presents the forehead of the famous image of Didarganj *Yakshi* of 3rd century B.C.

6. Necklace made of gold and green stone
 2700 B.C., Mohenjo-daro (Fig. 117)
 Gold, Green Linarite stone
 Diameter 4.5 Cm, Wt. 186.9 grain
 N. No. 274-91
 Acc. No. 49.254/18
 National Museum, New Delhi
 (D. P. Sharma: 2002)

Fig. 117 : Necklace, Gold and green stone. C. 2700 B.C. Mohenjodaro. Neg No. 274-91, Acc No. 49-254/18. National Museum, New Delhi Collection.

This is part of a necklace composed of 8 barrel-shaped light green jade beads and 26 double concave gold beads. Each jade bead is separated from the other by either three or five disc-shaped beads of gold. This is partly identical with the other green stone necklace from Mohenjo-daro, which is the other half portion of this necklace, and is now displayed in the National Museum of Pakistan.

7. Girdle (Belt)
   2700 B.C., Mohenjo-daro
   Red carnelian stone (Fig. 118)
   Length of each bead 9.6 cms, Dia. 5 cm
   Total length 90 cm including corner
   N. No. 247-91 & 253-91
   Acc. No. 49.244/144
   National Museum, New Delhi
   (D. P. Sharma: 2002)

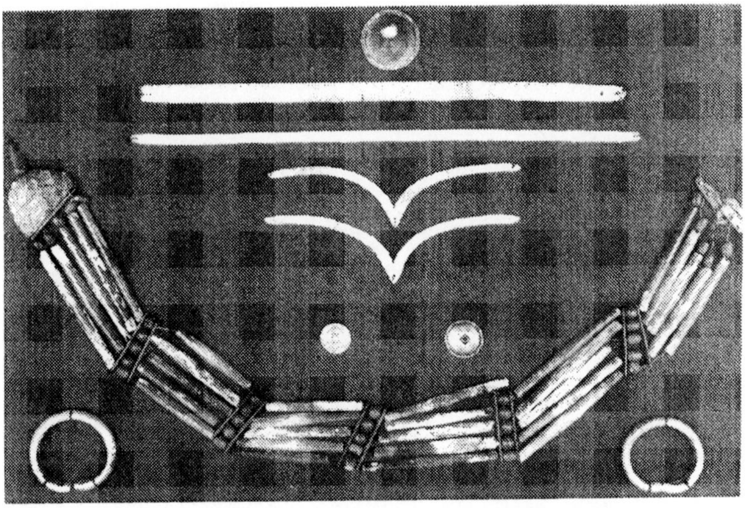

Fig. 118 : Girdle or Belt, C.2700 B.C. Mohenjodaro Red carnelian stone and silver. Neg No. 247-91, Acc. No. 49-244/144 (356) National Museum, New Delhi Collection.

This is a long girdle (Belt) made of thirty carnelian beads, which was fastened around the waist to keep the cloth (lower garment) of a female in tight position between the hips and rib part of the waist. Red carnelian beads are bi-conical or cylindrical in shape. Each bead is 9.6 cm in length and 5 cm diameter in the middle and bored in from each side. Sets of 5 carnelian beads are arranged in six parts in this belt. There are in total ten spacers of bronze in this belt, which are arranged in sets of two groups just after the five carnelian beads, which are in parallel row. The red carnelian beads have a covering of white steatite and this may be weathering erect. At each end of the carnelian bead there is a solid round bead of copper. At each end there is a bronze semi-circular terminal followed by a tube in which one is missing. A few carnelian beads are in pieces and one copper terminal is also damaged and another one is missing. Beads craftsmen of Harappans were importing carnelian nodules from Khambhat mines of Gujarat. The main source of carnelian and jasper stone appears to be Kathiawadi and a locality called Rajpipla near village Ratanpur and Khambhat. The semi-precious stone, carnelian is also available in other regions of Gujarat, Madhya Pradesh, upper Godavari region in Maharashtra and also in mines of Rajasthan. Rohri mines of Pakistan (Sindh) were the main source of chert and other semi-precious stone modules.

Harappan traders were also exporting red carnelian long cylindrical beads to regions of West Asia (Mesopotamia). Belts or necklace made of identical type of carnelian cylindrical beads were also reported from Allahdino and Nausharo-both mature Harappan sites. These are now in the collection of Pakistan. These are exactly identical with the belt of carnelian and copper beads from Mohenjo-daro which is housed now in the site Museum of Mohenjo-daro and also with two other belts from Allahdino and Nausharo, now in the collection of Department of Archaeology, Karachi. A similar type of long bi-conical or cylindrical beads of red carnelian stone was also reported from Kunal, Chanhudaro, Mohenjo-daro, Allahdino, Harappa, Lothal, Banawali, Kalibangan, Mandi, Dholavira and Rakhigarhi-all Harappan sites. Each of these beads measures 6.8 cm long (Fig. 119).

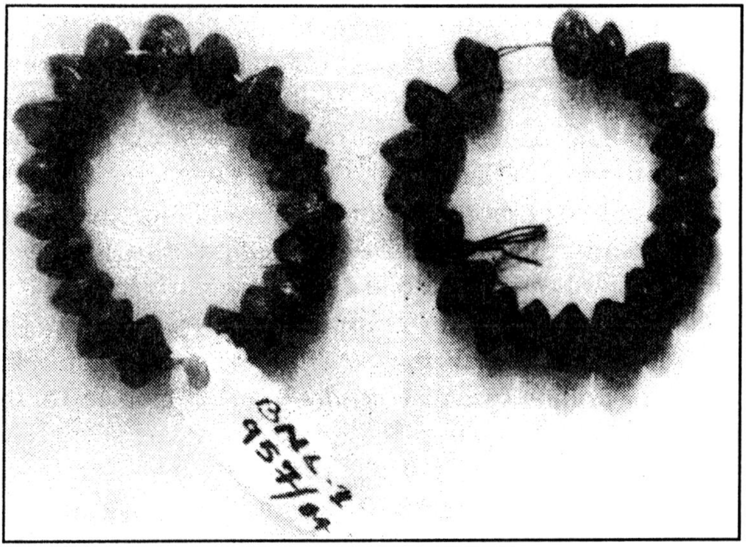

Fig. 119 : Two parts of one necklace, C.2600 B.C. Lapislazuli Banawali. Acc. No. BNL957/1, Neg No. 6/31-2000, A.S.I. Collection, New Delhi.

The perforation and drilling of these carnelian beads was done by the chipping technique and they were hardened by copper or cylindrical stone sticks. According to some authors stone drills for drilling these carnelian beads were made of the hardest and rare form of metamorphic rocks which artificial heating might have further modified. Stone drills of metamorphic rocks have been reported from Mohenjo-daro, Harappa, Dholavira and Chanhudaro. The earliest carnelian beads of the Harappan type have been reported from the deposits of early Harappan (circa 3000 B.C.) at Kunal and other sites. Besides this, terracotta imitations of long carnelian beads of the early Harappan period were also discovered in large numbers from Kunal and Mehrgarh.

Carnelian bead-making was a specialized craft activity of the mature Harappan. Ethnographic and experimental studies made by K. Bhan and Kenoyer in Khambat area have made it possible to reconstruct the basic process of manufacture of long cylindrical carnelian beads. First, a long nodule was brought from the Khambhat mines to the Harappan sites. After drying, these were heated at bead-making sites in a shallow oven to make the stones easier to saw. The large nodules were sawn length-wise to produce two or more segments that were then chipped to make beads rough out. These roughed-out carnelian beads might have been reheated to deepen the red colour. A shaft hammer was used for chipping very long-beads. The Harappan beads-makers used a fine-grained metamorphic drill for drilling carnelian beads. Some scholars are of the opinion that the mature Harappan craftsmen might have used a hand-held bow drill with the bead held firmly in a wooden vice. The whole process of drilling was done under water or at the site located near the river or sea or a tank. The carnelian beads discovered from Allahdino, Mohenjo-daro, Lothal and Dholavira ranging in length between 6 to 13 cm would have required between three to eight days of steady drilling for perforating them. Grinding on stone with sand later on polished them.

Terracotta necklaces and girdles of red colour, which are exactly identical with this carnelian necklace or belt, were reported from Mohenjo-daro. A few terracotta female figurines from Mohenjo-daro and Harappa are adorned with a similar type of necklaces and girdles. D.P. Sharma proposes that the Harappan people might have used this carnelian belt. As a girdle and also as a necklace.

8. Headband (Fig 120).
   2700 B.C., Mohenjo-daro Gold
   36.3 cm. x 1.4 cm, wt 63 grain
   N. No. 257-91, 4825-65
   Acc No. 49.244/6
   National Museum, New Delhi
   (D. P. Sharma: 2002)

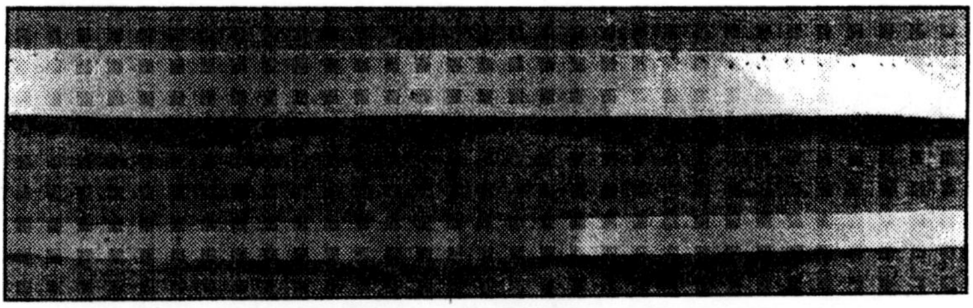

Fig. 120 : Flat headband, C.2700 B.C. Mohenjodaro, Gold. N. 4225-65, Acc No. 49-244/6, National Museum, New Delhi Collection.

This is a thin flat gold band or head ornament, which has two holes on either end for tying it with a thread. The fillet has the decoration of a punctuated design depicting the ritual pot or offering stand (disc on stand) which is a common Harappan motif generally found on the seals of the Mature Harappan period. This is identical in shape and decoration with the other gold fillet from Mohenjo-daro, which is now on display in the site Museum of Mohenjo-daro, Pakistan. The headband under reference is now in the collection of the National Museum, New Delhi. It is now on display in the jewellery gallery of the National Museum, New Delhi.

This ornament partly resembles another thin headband from Mohenjo-daro, which is also on display in the Jewellery gallery of the National Museum, New Delhi. A similar decorative fillet with adorns is on the forehead of the famous stone priest from Mohenjo-daro now housed in Karachi Museum, Pakistan. An identical headband recently discovered from Rakhigarhi is on display in the Harappan gallery of the National Museum, New Delhi.

Identical silver headbands or head ornaments have been reported from Allahdino and also from Kunal, Rakhigarhi, Dholavira and Mandi. Thin gold fillets or thin head ornaments appear to be a common feature of the decorative headdress worn by both men and women of the

Fig. 121 : Jewellery items from Mohenjodaro C.2700-2000 B.C. Gold, silver and semi-precious stone. Acc No. E-18, Neg No. 4821-65, National Museum, New Delhi Collection.

pre-Harappan and mature Harappan periods. They continued during the early historic period and are also found among the present-day population of south Asia. A few more carved male stone sculptures and terracotta female figurines from Mohenjo-daro also have a straight fillet around the forehead. This decorative head ornament was mostly made of silver, gold or other material and was tied with a cord at the back of the head. These two gold fillets from Mohenjo-daro with the depiction of a ritual pot or offering stands (Disc on stand) give us the impression that these items were probably used in some ritual by the mature Harappans. The depiction of such a ritual fillet on a priest's head confirms that he may be some god of the later Vedic period, most probably *Indra*. These two thin gold fillets from Mohenjo-daro have tiny holes all along the edge for attaching tiny beads or pendants. This is identical in shape with the curved hair fillet worn throughout by present-day South Asians. A few other jewellery items from Mohenjo-daro are on display in the Harappan gallery (Fig. 121). These Jewellery items are still in use by dancer and tribes of Rajasthan which shows Harappan legacy.

Appendices

Appendix - 1

Chronology of South Asia Region

Archaeological and Historical Events	*General Dates*
Australopithecus with stone pebble	4.4 MYA
· **Lower Palaeolithic**	
1. (Clactonion & Abbivillian)	+2MYA to 1MYA
2. Acheulian	1.2 to .3 Mya
Middle Palaeolithic (Mousterian)	300,000 to 40,000 b.p.
Upper Palaeolithic	40,000 to 10,000 b.p.
Epi-Palaeolithic	
'Mesolithic' Transition	10,000 to 8000 B.C.
Mesolithic Period	8000 - 5000 B.C. in main land. (India)

Early Food Production Era	
Neolithic at Mehrgarh & Cambay	Ca. 8000 to 5000 B.C.
Neolithic Main land*	Ca. 5000 to 3000 B.C.*
Chalcolithic Baluchistan	Ca. 5000-2800 B.C.
Harappan Vedic Tradition	
Vedic Age	Ca. 3500 - 2000 B.C.
Rigvedic Culture	Ca. 3500 - 3000 B.C.
Yajurvedic Culture	Ca. 3000 - 2700 B.C.
Atharvavedic Culture	Ca. 2700 - 2000 B.C.
Samavedic Culture	Ca. 2700 - 2300 B.C.
Early Harappan Phase	Ca. 3500 to 2800 B.C.
Neolithic in Mainland	Ca. 5000 - 2800 B.C.
Chalcolithic (Ahar) in Mainland of India (Rajasthan)	Ca. 3200 - 1800 B.C.
Mature Harappan Phase	Ca. 2700 to 2000 B.C.
Late Harappan phase	Ca. 1900 to 1500 B.C.
Beginning of Iron*	Ca. 2000 to 1400 B.C.
Copper-hoard & O.C.P.	Ca. 2800 to 1100 B.C.
Period of Rama	Ca. 1600 - 1500 B.C.
Painted Grey ware	Ca. 1600 - 600 B.C.
Period of Mahabharata	Ca. 1500 - 1400 B.C.
Northern Black Polished ware	Ca. 700 - 100 B.C.
Early Historic Period begins around Ca 600 B.C.	
Buddha (Siddhartha Gautama)	Ca. 563 - 483 B.C.
Panini (Sanskrit grammarian)	Ca. 500 - 400 B.C.

Historical Events	***General Dates***
Alexander of Macedon receives 'submission' and becomes the 'ally' of Ambhi, king of Texila,	326 B.C.
Mauryan Empire	Ca. 317 - 184 B.C.
Chandra Gupta Mauryan Empire	Ca. 317 - 298 B.C.
Kautilya or Vishnu Gupta (Minister of Chandra Gupta, author of Arthashastra)	Early Contemporary of Chandra Gupta. Ca. 317-298 B.C.
Bindusara	Ca. 298 - 274 B.C.
Ashoka	Ca. 274 - 232 B.C.
Samprat and Dasharath	Ca. 232 - 187 B.C.
Brahdratha	Ca. 187 - 184 B.C.
Sunga Kings	Ca. 184 B.C. - 100 B.C.
Mitra Rulers	Ca. 100 B.C. to 1 B.C.
Kusanas	Ca. 50 B.C. to 234 A.D.
Kujula Kadphises	First half of 1st C.A.D.
Vima Kadphises	58 A.D. to 78 A.D.
Kanishka I	78 A.D. - 101 A.D.
Huviska	106 A.D. - 140 A.D.
Vasudeva	142/45 A.D. (174-177A.D.)
Kanishka II	177 A.D. - 194 A.D.
Vasiska	199 A.D. - 205 A.D.
Kanishka III	205 A.D. - 218 A.D.
Vasudeva II	218 A.D. - 234 A.D.
Gupta Dynasty	319 A.D. to 578 A.D.
Harshavardhan	605 A.D. to 645 A.D.

*1. Earliest evidence of early man Australopithecus fossils goes back to 6 MYA.

*2. Earliest man-made stone tools (pebbles) were reported from Remedis in Ethiopia and these finds go back up to 4.4 million years back and in Sohan valley its date goes back to 2 Million years back.

*3. Early Achenlian or Abbivillian begins in Africa around 2-15 M.Y.A. Recent E.S.R. dates of Early Acheulian given by K. Paddaya from Husongi (India) go back to 1.2 M.Y.A. Hema Ragavan dated Bovi gravel up to 1.4. M.Y.A.

*4. Mousterian Acheulian tools of lower palaeolithic middle palaeolithic transition begin in Europe around. 3 M.Y.A. and in Patpara (India) around, 1.25 M.Y.A.

*5. Earliest date of copper metallurgy is from Mehrgarh, which goes back to C. 5000 B.C.

*6. Wheel-made pottery was known at Mehrgarh around circa C. 4000-3800 B.C.

*7. Iron was known at Gufkral around 1870 B.C. and at Dadupur Lahura-Deo and Malhar 1700 B.C. Iron was also reported from Allahdino and Ahar which can be dated up to 2000 B.C.

Appendix - 2

Radio-carbon dating

The post-War II thrust in scientific research has resulted in many discoveries benefitting mankind. Archaeology has also had its share. One of such benefits is the invaluable gift 'a means for absolute dating' the Radio-carbon dating method. During the quarter century many determinations (C^{14}) for Indian sites have been made and are now available. The dates are the outcome of hard and careful work at many laboratories in India, viz. T.I.F.R. Bombay now at PRL Ahmedabad and Birbal Sahni Institute of Palaeobotany at Lucknow. The dates are based on the Radio-carbon half-life value of 5730±40 years. Initially, the half-life value was 70 years, but later the former was adopted universally. Here, the dates based on the half-life value 5568, have been converted to the dates corresponding to the half-life value 5730 plus 40 years, for uniformity and for easy reference. The year 1950 is a base year for conversion into BC / AD scales.

The dates cover three cultures:

(1) Early Harappan,

(2) Mature Harappan,

(3) Late Harappan.

c^{14} dates of Harappan Sites

Site	No.	5568 BP	5730 BC	Calibration	Cultural Association	Date List
1	2	3	4	5	6	7
Allahdino	P.2296	3930+50 BP	2100+53 BP	2555-2325 BC	Urban Harappan	PENN XIX
-do-	P.2237	3840+6B P	2010+63 BC	2415-2185 BC	-do-	POSSEHL(197)
-do-	P.2295	3760+70 BP	1930+73 BC	2230-2125 BC	-do-	-do-
Amri	TF.864	4710+110 BP	2900+113 BC	3660-3665 BC	Pd.IB	TATA VIII
-do-	TF.863	4485+110 BP	2670+113 BC	3375-3020 BC	Pd.IC	TATA VIII
Balakot	HAR 1992	4050+130 BP	2322+1350 BC	2890-2510 BC	Pd.II.Urban Surface	
-do-	HAR 1993	3890+100 BP	2057+1050 BC	2560-1965 BC	-do-	
Banawali	PRL 205	3810+180 BC	1975+185 BC	2560-1965 BC	Pd.II. Urban Phase	PRLII
-do-	PRL 203	3800+150 BP	1965+155 BC	2425-1995 BC	-do-	PRLII
-do-	PRL 204	3260+120 BP	1410+ 125	1700-1415 BC	-do-	PRLII
Bara	TF 1205	3730+95 BP	1890+98 BC	2330-1975 BC	Pd.I Early Harappan Lower level	TATA X

After Sudha Satawadi 1994

c^{14} dates of Harappan Site

1	2	3	4	5	6	7
Banawali	*TF 1204*	*3690+150 BP*	*1850+155 BC*	*2355-1885 BC*	*Pd.I.Early (Upper level)*	*TATA*
-do-	*TF 1207*	*3490+85 BP*	*1945+88 BC*	*1980-1690 BC*	*-do-*	*TARA X*
-do-	*TF 1206*	*3135+100 BP*	*1280+103 BC*	*1585-1330 BC*	*Pd.IEarly (Lower-level)*	*TATA X*
Burzahom	*TF 128*	*4205+115 BP*	*2381+120 BC*	*2980-2655 BC*	*Pd.IB.Neolithic*	*TATA III*
-do-	*TF 123*	*4055+115 BP*	*2227+120 BC*	*2870-2525 BC*	*Pd.I.A. Neolithic*	*TATA III*
-do-	*TF 127*	*3935+115 BP*	*2103+120 BC*	*2645-3210 BC*	*Pd.IB.Neolithic*	*TATA III*
-do-	*TF 14*	*3860+340 BP*	*2026+350 BC*	*?*	*Neolithic*	*TATA III*
-do-	*TF 13*	*3690+125 BP*	*1850+129 BC*	*2185-1740 BC*	*Pd.I.A. Neolithic*	*TATA III*
-do-	*TF 129*	*3670+90 BP*	*1830+93 BC*	*2215-1900 BC*	*Neolithic*	*TATA IV*
-do-	*TF 15*	*3390+105 BP*	*1540+108 BC*	*1880-1595 BC*	*Pd.IB. Neolithic*	*TATA I*
Daimabad	*BS 176*	*3590+90 BP*	*1950+93 BC*	*2160-1850 BC*	*Pd.I.Savalda*	*BS. III*
-do-	*PRL 655*	*3490+110 BP*	*1645+113 BC*	*1980-1690 BC*	*Pd.III Buff & cream ware*	*PRL V*
-do-	*PRL 654*	*3460+100 BP*	*1615+103 BC*	*1850-1645 BC*	*-do-*	*PRL IV*
-do-	*BS 177*	*3460+110 BP*	*1615+103 BC*	*1910-1555 BC*	*Pd.I.Savalda*	*PRL IV*
-do-	*PRL 428*	*3400+110 BP*	*1552+115 BC*	*1910-1555 BC*	*Pd.I Savalda*	*PRL V*
-do-	*PRL 429*	*3390+150 BP*	*1540+155 BC*	*1880-1595 BC*	*Pd.II Post-urban*	*BSIII*
-do-	*BS 180*	*3390+100 B*	*1540-103 BC*			

After Sudha Satawadi 1994

c^{14} dates of Harappan Site

1	2	3	4	5	6	7
Damb Sadaat	*P522*	*4378+196 BP*	*2560+202 BC*	*3370-2865 BC*	*D.S.II*	*PENN VI*
-do-	*L 180 C*	*4375+412 BP*	*2556+425 BC*	*3370-2865 BC*	*D.S.II*	*LAMONT*
-do-	*L180 E*	*4367+361 BP*	*2548+372 BC*	*3370-2865 BC*	*D.S.II*	*LAMONT*
-do-	*L180 B*	*4338+350 BP*	*2518+361 BC*	*3365-2785 BC*	*D.S.I*	*LAMONT*
-do-	*UW 59*	*4330+70 BP*	*2510+72 BC*	*3155-2895 BC*	*D.S.I*	*UW III*
-do-	*UW 60*	*4030+160 BP*	*2200+165 BC*	*2880-2395 BC*	*D.S.III*	*UW III*
-do-	*P523*	*4020+74 BP*	*2200+76 BC*	*2665-2530 BC*	*D.S.II*	*PENN.VI*
Jhunkar	*P 2476*	*4630+300 BP*	*2820+300 BC*	*3660-3140 BC*	*Jhukar?*	*PENN VI*
Jhodhpura	*PRL 275*	*4360+160 BP*	*2540+165 BC*	*3360-2880 BC*	*Black & Red ware*	*PRL III*
-do-	*PRL 278*	*4060+170 BP*	*2230+175 BC*	*2895-2515 BC*	*OCP*	*PRL III*
Kalibangan	*TF 155*	*4195+115 BP*	*2370+118 BC*	*2980-2655 BC*	*Pd.I, Early Harappan*	*TATA IV*
-do-	*TF 157*	*4120+110 BP*	*2295+113 BC*	*2900-2615 BC*	*-do-*	*TATA III*
-do-	*TF241*	*4090+90 BP*	*2265+93 BC*	*2890-2540 BC*	*-do-*	*TATA IV*
-do-	*TF160*	*4060+100 BC*	*2230+103 BC*	*2875-2530 BC*	*Pd.II Urban Harappan*	*TATA III*
-do-	*TF 942*	*4055+110 BP*	*2225+113 BC*	*2875-2530 BC*	*-do-*	*TATA VIII*
-do-	*TF 162*	*3940+100 BP*	*2110+103 BC*	*2645-2310 BC*	*Pd.I.Early Harappan*	*TATA*
-do-	*TF 607*	*3930+120 BP*	*2100+124 BC*	*2646-2310 BC*	*Pd.I.Early Harappan*	*TATA III*

After Sudha Satawadi 1994

c^{14} dates of Harappan Site

1	2	3	4	5	6	7
Kalibangan	TF 25	3930+110 BP	2100+113 BC	2645-2310 BC	Pd.II.Urban-do-	TATA I
-do-	TF 161	3930+100 BP	2100+103 BC	2645-2310 BC	Pd.I.Early Harappan	TATA III
-do-	TF 153	3910+110 BP	2075+113 BC	2635-2300 BC	Pd.II.Urban-do-	TATA VI
-do-	TF 608	3910+110 BP	2075+113 BC	2635-2300 BC	-do-	TATA V
-do-	TF 163	3910+100 BP	2075+103 BC	3635-2300 BC	-do-	TATA III
-do-	TF 145	3890+100 BP	2060+103 BC	2560-2295 BC	-do-	TATA II
-do-	TF 481	3879+72 BP	2045+74 BC	2425-2300 BC	-do-	PENN VI
-do-	TF 147	3865+100 BP	2030+103 BC	2440-2180 BC	-do-	TATA II
-do-	TF 948	3815+100 BP	1980+103 BC	2420-2145 BC	-do-	TATA VIII
-do-	TF 605	3810+105 BP	1975+108 BC	2415-2135 BC	-do-	TATA V
-do-	TF 165	3800+100 BP	1965+103 BC	2415-2130 BC	Pd.I.Early Harappan	TATA III
-do-	TF 151	3800+100 BP	1965+103 BC	2415-2130 BC	Pd.II.Urban	TATA II
-do-	TF 139	3775+100 BP	1940+103 BC	2410-2105 BC	-do-	TATA III
-do-	TF 947	3765+85 BP	1930+83 BC	2405-2020 BC	-do-	TATA VIII
-do-	TF 156	3740+105 BP	1900+108 BC	2340-1980 BC	Pd.I.Early Harappan	TATA VI
-do-	TF 150	3740+100 BP	1900+103 BC	2340-1980 BC	Pd.II.Urban-do-	TATA II
-do-	TF 141	3705+110 BP	1865+113 BC	2320-1955 BC	Pd.II.Urban-do-	TATA IV
-do-	TF 149	3675+140 BP	1835+114 BC	2325-1880 BC	-do-	TATA IV
-do-	TF 154	3665+110 BP	1025+113 BC	2215-1900 BC	Pd.I.Early Harappan	TATA III
-do-	TF 142	3635+100 BP	1795+103 BC	2190-1880 BC	Pd.II Urban -do-	TATA IV

After Sudha Satawadi 1994

c^{14} dates of Harappan Sites

1	2	3	4	5	6	7
Kalibangan	*TF 152*	*3615+85 BP*	*1775+88 BC*	*2180-1870 BC*	*Pd. II urban*	*TATA IV*
-do-	*TF 240*	*3610+110 BP*	*1770+113 BC*	*2170-1865 BC*	*Pd.I.Early Harappan*	*TATA IV*
-do-	*TF 946*	*3605+100 BP*	*1765+103 BC*	*2170-1865 BC*	*-do-*	
					II.Urban -do-	*TATA VIII*
-do-	*TF 143*	*3510+110 BP*	*1665+113 BC*	*2000-1700 BC*	*-do-*	*TATA IV*
-do-	*TF244*	*3250+90 BP*	*1400+93 BC*	*1665-1419 BC*	*-do-*	*TATA IV*
-do-	*TF138*	*3075+100 BP*	*1217+105 BC*	*1540-1240 BC*	*-do-*	*TATA IV*
-do-	*TF 957*	*2355+200 BP*	*475+205 BC*	*785-180 BC*	*Pd.I.Early Harappan*	*TATA IX*
Kot Diji	*P 196*	*4421+141 BP*	*2605+145 BC*	*3370-2900 BC*	*Kot Dijian*	*PENN III*
-do-	*P 179*	*4161+151 BP*	*2335+156 BC*	*2980-2545 BC*	*-do-(Lower town)*	*PENN III*
-do-	*P 180*	*4083+137 BP*	*2255+141 BC*	*2900-2525 BC*	*-do-*	*PENN III*
-do-	*P 195*	*3925+134 BP*	*2095+138 BC*	*2660-2190 BC*	*-do-(Latest levels)*	*PENN III*
Kile Gul Mohammad	*L180A*	*5497+500 BP*	*3712+515 BC*	*4555-4090 BC*	*KGM I*	*LAMONT*
-do-	*P 52A*	*5474+83 BP*	*3690+85 BC*	*4435-4120 BC*	*KGM I*	*PENN VI*
-do-	*UW61*	*5260+80 BP*	*3470+82 BC*	*4165-3885 BC*	*KGM I*	*UW III*
Lothal	*TF 136*	*3915+130 BP*	*2880+134 BC*	*2655-2185 BC*	*Pd.IA (Lothal A)*	*TATA III*
-do-	*TF 22*	*3845+110 BP*	*2010+113 BC*	*2430-2165 BC*	*Pd.IIIB (Lothal A)*	*TATA I*
-do-	*TF 26*	*3830+120 BP*	*1995+124 BC*	*2425-2155 BC*	*-do-*	*TATA I*

After Sudha Satawadi 1994

c^{14} dates of Harappan Sites

1	2	3	4	5	6	7
Lothal	TF 133	3740+110 BP	1900+113 BC	2340-1980 BC	Pd.IIA (Lothal A)	TATA III
-do-	TF 29	3705+105 BP	1900+113 BC	2340-1980 BC	Pd.IVA (Lothal A)	TATA I
-do-	TF 23	3705+105 BP	1865+100 BC	2320-1955 BC	Pd.VA (Lothal B)	TATA I
-do-	TF 19	3650+135 BP	1810+139 BC	2315-1865 BC	Pd.VA (Lothal B)	TATA I
-do-	TF 135	3405+125 BP	1555+129 BC	1950-1570 BC	Pd.IIA (Lothal A)	TATA III
Mehrgarh	BETA 2689	6500+78 BP	4745+80 BC	-5555-5255BC	Pd.III	
-do-	BETA 1712	9385+120 BP	7717+125 BC	8215-7215 BC	Pd.IA	
-do-	LY 1950	8440+250 BP	6745+258 BC	N.A.	Pd.I.B	LYONI
-do-	BETA 1407	7115+290 BP	5378+300 BC	6360-5470 BC	Pd.I.A	
-do-	BETA1720	7115+120 BP	5378+125 BC	6200-5625 BC	Pd.IIA?	
-do-	BETA1408	6925+80 BP	5183+80 BC	5590-5480 BC	Pd.IA	
-do-	LY994	6290+70 BP	4529+70 BC	5325-5095 BC	Pd.IB	
-do-	LY993	6110+90 BP	4343+90 BC	5240-4925 BC	Pd.IB	
-do-	LY908	6090+70 BP	4323+70 BC	5215-4930 BC	Pd.IB	
-do-	907	6020+80 BP	4050+82 BC	5195-4875 BC	Pd.IB	LABDE CHIMIE
Mehrgarh	LY 906	5950+65 BP	4180+67 BC	5055-4735 BC	Pd.IB	-do-
-do-	LY 909	5940+55 BP	4170+57 BC	5040-4730 BC	Pd.IB	-do-
-do-	LY 910	5880+100 BP	4105+196 BC	4975-4565 BC	Pd.IA	-do-
-do-	LY 1947	5830+190 BP	4055+196 BC	5020+4440 BC	Pd.IA	LYONI
-do-	LY 1948	5720+730 BP	3940+152 BC	4910-4410 BC	Pd.IA	LYONI
-do-	LY 1949	5530+180 BP	3745+185 BC	4560-4110 BC	Pd.IA	LYONI
-do-	LY 1945	5560+310 BP	3571+320 BC	4545-3795 BC	Pd.IIB	

After Sudha Satawadi 1994

c^{14} dates of Harappan Sites

1	2	3	4	5	6	7
Mehrgarh	*LY 1528*	*4190+140 BP*	*2366+145 BC*	*3025-2635 BC*	*Pd.IV*	
-do-	*LY 1529*	*3960+140 BP*	*2129+145 BC*	*2670-2300 BC*	*Pd.VI-VII*	
-do-	*LY 1527*	*3510+130 BP*	*1727+135 BC*	*2175-1715 BC*	*Pd.VI-VII*	
-do-	*BETA 1719*	*1340+125 BP*	*1179+130 BC*	*12790-10790 BC*	*Pd.IA*	
Mitathal	*PRL 292*	*4210+210 BP*	*2385+216 BC*	*3155-2610 BC*	*Pd.IB. Punja (Post Urban Phase)*	*PRL III*
-do-	*PRL 290*	*3820+130 BP*	*1985+134 BC*	*2435-205 BC*	*Pd.I.Urban Phase*	*PRL III*
-do-	*PRL 291*	*3600+110 BP*	*1760+113 BC*	*2165-1860 BC*	*Pd.IIA. Urban Phase*	*PRL III*
Mohenjo-daro	*P 1177*	*3985+64 BP*	*2155+65 BC*	*2650-2520 BC*	*Urban Phase*	*PENN X*
-do-	*P 1179*	*3913+64 BP*	*2080+66 BC*	*2545-2315 BC*	*-do-*	*-do-*
-do-	*P 1180*	*3828+60 BP*	*1995+63 BC*	*2415-2425 BC*	*-do-*	*-do-*
-do-	*P 1178A*	*3802+59 BP*	*1965+61 BC*	*2405-2155 BC*	*-do-*	*-do-*
-do-	*P 1176*	*3801+59 BP*	*1965+61 BC*	*4505-2155 BC*	*-do-*	*-do-*
-do-	*P 1182*	*3702+63 BP*	*1865+66 BC*	*2210-1975 BC*	*-do-*	*-do-*
-do-	*TF 75*	*3600+110 BP*	*1760+113 BC*	*2165-1360 BC*	*Jhukar levels? Date Pavement 1.27M.*	*TATA II*
Mundigak	*TF 1129*	*4950+105 BP*	*3150+108 BC*	*3885-3685 BC*	*Pd.I (2-3)*	*TATA X*
-do-	*TF 1132*	*4805+110 BP*	*3000+103 BC*	*3690-3495 BC*	*Pd.I (5) or II (1)*	*TATA X*
-do-	*TF 1131*	*4570+100 BP*	*2755+103 BC*	*3390-3155 BC*	*Pd.I (5)*	*TATA X*
-do-	*GSY 53*	*4185+150 BC*	*2361+155 BC*	*3015-2630 BC*	*Pd.III (5)*	
-do-	*GSY 50*	*3945+150 BP*	*2113+155 BC*	*2660-2290 BC*	*Pd.I (5)*	

After Sudha Satawadi 1994

c^{14} dates of Harappan Sites

1	2	3	4	5	6	7
Mundigak	GSY 52	3480+115 BP	1634+120 BC	1975-1685 BC	Pd.II (1)-do-	GSY 27
-do-	GSY 75	3600+110 BP	1760+113 BC	2165-1860 BC	Pd.III (1)	
Nindowari	TF 862	3900+150 BP	2065+108 BC	2560-2295 BC	Pd.II or III Kulli	TATA VIII
Rehmandheri	PRL 679	3100	N.A.	N.A.	N.D.	PRL V
-do-	PRL 676	4520+110 BP	2705+113 BC	33-803040 BC	Pre-Kot Dijian	PRL V
-do-	PRL 675	4400+110 BP	2580+113 BC	3650-2910 BC	-do-	PRL V
-do-	WIS 1697	4300+70 BP	2479+70 BC	3055-2885 BC	-do-	
-do-	WIS 1698	4190+70 BP	2360+70 BC	2920-2775 BC	-do-	
-do-	WIS 1699	4180+70 BP	2355+70 BC	2910-2765 BC	Pd.II.Early Kot Dijian	
-do-	WIS 1700	4070+90 BP	2242+90 BC	2880-2533 BC	-do-	
-do-	PRL 674	4000+150 BP	2170+155 BC	2865-2320 BC	-do-	PRL V
-do-	PRL 673	3900+130 BP	2065+134 BC	2650-2170 BC	Pd.III.Late Kot Dijian	PRL V
-do-	WIS 1701	3850+70 BP	2015+70 BC	2420-2190 BC	-do-	
-do-	BM 2026	3730+50 BP	1890+50 BC	2315-2010 BC	-do-	BM XVI
-do-	WIS 1702	3620+80 BP	1779+80 BC	2180-1870 BC	-do-	
-do-	BM 2067	3580+110 BP	1735+113 BC	2150-1770 BC	-do-	BMX VI
Rojdi	PRL 1085	4020+105 BP	2190+108 BC	2680-2515 BC	Rojdi A 45K	PRL
-do-	PRL 1087	4010+110 BP	2180+115 BC	2675-2575 BC	-do-	PRL
-do-	PRL 1283	3980+100 BP	2140+100 BC	2660-2385 BC	Rojdi A 46L	PRL
-do-	PRL 1093	3920+110 BP	2088+115 BC	2640-2305 BC	Rojdi A 45	PRL
-do-	PRL 1083	3875+125 BP	2040+130 BC	2640-2160 BC	Rojdi B 76L	PRL

After Sudha Satawadi 1994

c^{14} dates of Harappan Sites

1	2	3	4	5	6	7
Rojdi	*PRL 1089*	*3865+115 BP*	*2030+120 BC*	*2240-2180 BC*	*Rojdi A 45K*	*PRL*
-do-	*TF200*	*3810+110 BP*	*1975+113 BC*	*2415-2135 BC*	*Pd.I.Phase B*	*TATA III*
-do-	*PRL 1284*	*3810+110 BP*	*1980+100 BC*	*2415-2135 BC*	*Rojdi A 46L*	*PRL*
-do-	*PRL 1088*	*3767+125 BP*	*1930+130 BC*	*2420-1970 BC*	*Rojdi B 45K*	*PRL*
-do-	*PRL 1285*	*3740+140 BP*	*1900+145 BC*	*2410-1945 BC*	*Rojdi A 46L*	*PRL*
-do-	*PRL 1084*	*3700+145 BP*	*1860+150 BC*	*1350-1890 BC*	*Rojdi C 76L*	*PRL*
-do-	*F199*	*3590+100 BP*	*1750+103 BC*	*2150-1850 BC*	*Pd.I.Phase B*	*TATA III*
-do-	*PRL 1281*	*3520+110 BP*	*1680+110 BC*	*2015-1710 BC*	*Rojdi B. 46L*	*PRL*
-do-	*1282*	*3470+140 BP*	*1620+145 BC*	*2000-1665 BC*	*Rojdi B. 46L*	*PRL*
Hulas						
Saharan-pur (w.U.P.)	*PRL 1032*	*4380+150*			*Late Harappan*	
-do-	*PRL 1031*	*3840+110*			*-do-*	
Sanghol	*PRL 511*	*3740+160 BP*	*1900+165 BC*	*2410-1945 BC*	*Pd.I Post Urban Late Harappan*	*PRL IV*
-do-	*PRL 509*	*3570+150 BP*	*1725+155 BC*	*2175-1700 BC*	*-do-*	*PRL IV*
-do-	*PRL 510*	*3550+150 BP*	*1705+155 BC*	*2160-1700 BC*	*-do-*	*PRL IV*
-do-	*PRL513*	*3540+150 BP*	*1695+155 BC*	*2155-1695 BC*	*-do-*	*PRL IV*
Shortughai	*MC 1730*	*3534+92 BP*	*1690+92 BC*	*2100-1720 BC*	*Pd.IV. Post Urban*	
-do-	*NY521*	*3432+160 BP*	*1585+165 BC*	*1965-1590 BC*	*-do-*	

After Sudha Satawadi 1994

c^{14} dates of Harappan Sites

1	2	3	4	5	6	7
Surkotada	PRL 85	4140+130 BP	2315+134 BC	2940-2540 BC	UN.K.	PRL I
-do-	TF 1305	3890+95 BP	2055+98 BC	2555-2285 BC	Pd.IA Uppertown	TATA X
Surkotada	TF 1301	3840+130 BP	2005+134 BC	2550-2125 BC	UNK	TATA XI
-do-	TF 1310	3810+95 BP	1975+98 BC	2415-2135 BC	Pd.IA	TATA X
-do-	TF 1295	3780+95 BP	1945+98 BC	2410-2105 BC	Pd.IA. Lower town	TATA X
-do-	TF 1304/a	3645+90 BP	1805+93 BC	2195-1885 BC	Pd.IB. Upper town	TATA X
-do-	TF 1297	3665+95 BP	1795+98 BC	2190-1880 BC	Pd.IC	TATA X
-do-	TF 1311	3625+90 BP	1785+93 BC	2185-1875 BC	Pd.IC.	TATA X
-do-	TF 1294	3620+95 BP	1780+98 BC	2180-1875 BC	Pd.IC.	TATA X
-do-	TF 1307	3510+105 BP	1665+108 BC	2000-1700 BC	Pd.IC.	TATA X

After Sudha Satawadi 1994

c^{14} dates of Harappan Sites

Site	Number	5568 B.P.	5730 B.C.	Calibrated	Cultural Period
Loteshwar	***PRL 1564***	***4460 ± 110 B.P.***	***2510 ± 110 B.C.***	***2921 B.C.***	***Period II - Anarta Tradition***
Loteshwar	*PRL 1565*	*5050 ± 110 B.P.*	*3100 ± 110 B.C.*	*3698 B.C.*	*Period II - Anarta Tradition*
Padri	*PRL 1785*	*4390 ± 90 B.P.*	*4520 ± 90 B.C.*	*3048 B.C.*	*Period I - Padri Ware*
Padri	*PRL 1787*	*4820 ± 100 B.P.*	*4860 ± 100 B.C.*	*3680 B.C.*	*Period I - Padri Ware*
Prabhas Patan	*PRL 90*	*4240 ± 110 B.P.*	*2415 ± 115 B.C.*	*2892 B.C.*	*Period I - Pre Prabhas*
Prabhas Patan	*TF 1287*	*4280 ± 105 B.P.*	*2460 ± 110 B.C.*	*2911 B.C.*	*Period I - Pre Prabhas*
Rojdi	*PRL 1248*	*3810 ± 100 B.P.*	*1960 ± 105 B.C.*	*2283 B.C.*	*Period A - Sorath Harappan*
Rojdi	*PRL 1093*	*2920 ± 110 B.P.*	*2090 ± 115 B.C.*	*2462 B.C.*	*Period A - Sorath Harappan*
Rojdi	*PRL 1085*	*4020 ± 110 B.P.*	*2190 ± 115 B.C.*	*2573 B.C.*	*Period A - Sorath Harappan*
Rojdi	*PRL 1091*	*4150 ± 110 B.P.*	*2325 ± 115 B.C.*	*2667, 2699 B.C.*	*Period A - Sorath Harappan*
Rojdi	*PRL 1282*	*3470 ± 140 B.P.*	*1620 ± 145 B.C.*	*1866, 1772 B.C.*	*Period B - Sorath Harappan*
Rojdi	*PRL 1088*	*3770 ± 120 B.P.*	*1935 ± 125 B.C.*	*2198, 2149 B.C.*	*Period B - Sorath Harappan*
Rojdi	*TF 200*	*3810 ± 110 B.P.*	*1975 ± 115 B.C.*	*2283 B.C.*	*Period B - Sorath Harappan*
Lothal	*TF 27*	*3840 ± 110 B.P.*	*2005 ± 115 B.C.*	*2315 B.C.*	*Period A - Urban Harappan*
Lothal	*TF 22*	*3845 ± 110 B.P.*	*2010 ± 115 B.C.*	*2328 B.C.*	*Period A - Urban Harappan*
Lothal	*TF 136*	*3915 ± 130 B.P.*	*2808 ± 135 B.C.*	*2461 B.C.*	*Period A - Urban Harappan*
Lothal	*TF 19*	*3650 ± 135 B.P.*	*1810 ± 140 B.C.*	*2034 B.C.*	*Period B - Post Urban Harappan*
Kuntasi	*PRL 1371*	*3650 ± 140 B.P.*	*1810 ± 145 B.C.*	*2014 B.C.*	*Period I - Urban Harappan*
Kuntasi	*PRL 1370*	*3710 ± 160 B.P.*	*1870 ± 165 B.C.*	*2135, 2050 B.C.*	*Period I - Urban Harappan*
Kuntasi	*BS 567*	*3870 ± 90 B.P.*	*2035 ± 95 B.C.*	*2451, 2365 B.C.*	*Period I - Urban Harappan*
Nagwada	*A 4555*	*3700 ± 80 B.P.*	*1860 ± 80 B.C.*	*2133, 2067 B.C.*	*Period IB - Urban Harappan*
Vagad	*BS 752*	*3625 ± 100 B.P.*	*1780 ± 105 B.C.*	*2170 B.C.*	*Period IA - Urban Harappan*
Vagad	*BS 751*	*2320 ± 100 B.P.*	*1470 ± 105 B.C.*	*1775 B.C.*	*Period IB - Post- Urban Harappan*
Ahar	*TF 32*	*3400 ± 105 B.P.*	*1550 ± 110 B.C.*	*1733-1697 B.C.*	*Period IC - Banas Chalcolithic*
Navdatoli	*P 204*	*3449 ± 127 B.P.*	*1600 ± 130 B.C.*	*1749 B.C.*	*Period III - Malwa Chalcolithic*

After Sudha Satawadi 1994

Some Calibrated radiocarbon dates of the Early Harappan-I (3500-2800 B. C).

Site	*Sample No.*	*Calibrated Radiocarbon*	*Dates*
Balakot	*UCLA 1923A*	*4150-3800*	*B.C.*
	" 1923C	*3800-3520*	*B.C.*
	" 1923D	*3005-2765*	*B.C.*
Damb Sadaat (Period I)	*L-180 B*	*3515*	*B.C.*
Damb Sadaat (Period II)	*P-522*	*3370*	*B.C.*
-do-	*L180 C*	*3650*	*B.C.*
-do-	*L-180 E*	*3021-2927*	*B.C.*
Harappa	*BETA-33874*	*3338-3203*	*B.C.*
-do-	*WIS 2142*	*2863-2812*	*B.C.*
Jhukar	*P-2476*	*3785-2935*	*B.C.*
Kile-Gul-Md. (Period III a)	*UW-61*	*4165-3885*	*B.C.*
Loteshwar	*PRL-1565*	*3698*	*B.C.*
Mehrgarh (Pd.IA)	*BETA-1721*	*2812-7215*	*B.C.*
-do- (Period IV)	*LY-1528*	*3025-2635*	*B.C.*
Padri	*PRL-1787*	*3680*	*B.C.*
Rehman Dheri (Period I)	*PRL-675*	*3360-2910*	*B.C.*
-do-.	*PRL-676*	*3380-3143*	*B.C.*
Rana Ghundai (Period III a)	*P-2149*	*3390-3345*	*B.C.*
Rehman Dheri	*PRL-676*	*3331-3147*	*B.C.*
Sarai Khola (Period I)	*BM-1944*	*3334-3148*	*B.C.*

After Possehl 2000

Some Calibrated radiocarbon dates of the Early Harappan-II (3000 B.C.-2700 B.C.)

Site	***Sample No.***	***Calibrated Radiocarbon***	***Dates***
Gumla (Pd. II)	—	*2883-2784*	
Ghazi Shah	*BETA-33358*	*2867-2772*	
Harappa	*WIS-2142*	*2863-2726*	*B.C.*
-do-	*WIS-2140*	*2913*	*B.C.*
Hulas	*PRL-1032*	*3028-2930*	*B.C.*
Islam Chauki	*OKA-1005*	*2870-2774*	*B.C.*
Jhang	*BM-2201R*	*2903*	*B.C.*
Jodhapura			
(Ganeshwar Culture)	*PRL-275*	*3018-2926*	*B.C.*
Kalibangan (Pd.I)	*TF-155*	*2950-2650*	*B.C.*
-do-	*TF-141*	*2853-2882*	*B.C.*
-do-	*TF-155*	*2879-2709*	*B.C.*
Kot Diji	*P-196*	*3370-2900*	*B.C.*
-do-	*P-179*	*2980*	*B.C.*
Kunal (Pd.I)	*BETA-77727*	*3016*	*B.C.*
-do-(Pd. I, middle)	*BETA-77726*	*2837*	*B.C.*
Rehman Dheri	*PRL-676*	*3380-3040*	*B.C.*
-do- (Pd.II)	*WIS-1700*	*2800*	*B.C.*
Sarai Khola	*BM-1940*	*3360-2885*	*B.C.*
Somnath (Pd.I)	*TF-1287*	*3055-2800*	*B.C.*
Tarai Kala Dheri	*BM-1695*	*2875*	*B.C.*

After Possehl 2000

Radio Carbon Dates from Early Harappan Chalcolithic Sites of Gujarat

Site	Period	Culture	Lab no	5568 bp	5730 B.C.	Calibration	Reference
Padi	*Period III*		*PRL 1785*	*4390±90*	*4520±90*	*3048 BC*	*Shinde (1998)*
			PRL 1787	*4820±100*	*4960±100*	*3680 BC*	*do-*
Prabhas Patan and	*Period I*	*Pre-Prabhas*	*PRL 90*	*4240±110*	*2415±155*	*2982 BC*	*Dhavalikar and Possehl (1992)*
			TF 1287	*1280±105*	*2460±110*	*2911 BC*	*-do-*
Rojdi	*Rojdi A*	*Sorath Harappan*		*PRL 1089*	*3865±115*	*2035±125*	*2640-2150 BC Possehl and Raval (1989)*
			PRL 1093	*3920±105*	*2090±115*	*2645-2310 BC*	*-do-*
			PRL 1087	*4010±105*	*2180±115*	*2680-2515 BC*	*-do-*
			PRL 1085	*4020±105*	*2190±115*	*2680-2515 BC*	*-do-*
			PRL 1285	*3740±140*	*1900±145*	*2410-1945 BC*	*-do-*
			PRL 1284	*3810±100*	*1980±105*	*2415-2135 BC*	*-do-*
			PRL 1283	*3980±100*	*2140±105*	*2650-2385 BC*	*-do-*
Loteshwar	*Period II*	*Anartha*	*PRL 1564*	*4460±110*	*2510±110*	*2921 BC*	*Sonawane and Ajithprasad (1994)*
			PRL 1565	*5050±110*	*3100±110*	*3698 BC*	*-do-*

After Possehl 2000

Some calibrated dates of the Mature Harappan Civilization (2700 B.C.-2000 B.C.)

Site	*Sample No.*	*Calibrated Radiocarbon Dates*	
	(In Bolan-Saraswati Divide)		
Banawali	*PRL-205*	*2560-1965*	*B.C.*
Harappa	*WIS-2152*	*2863,2776*	*B.C.*
-do-	*WIS-2140*	*2913*	*B.C.*
Kalibangan (Pd. II)	*TF-160*	*2875-2530*	*B.C.*
-do-	*TF-152*	*1923*	*B.C.*
Mitathal	*PRL-290*	*2435-2095*	*B.C.*
Mohenjo-daro	*P-1179*	*2545-2315*	*B.C.*
-do-	*TF-1182 A*	*2210-1975*	*B.C.*
Nausharo	*BETA-18843*	*2598*	*B.C.*
Pirak (Pd.I)	*LY-1641*	*2647-2245*	*B.C.*
Rehman Dheri (Pd. III)	*PRL-673*	*2650-2170*	*B.C*
	(In Afghanistan Region)		
Shortughai	*NY-430*	*2651, 2610*	*B.C.*
-do-	*NY-425*	*2580*	*B.C.*
Said Kala Tepe	*DIC-18*	*255-1960*	*B.C.*
-do-	*DIC-22*	*2310-1720*	*B.C.*
	(In Gujarat Region)		
Lothal (Pd.A)	*TF-136*	*2655-2185*	*B.C.*
-do- (Pd.B)	*TF-19*	*2315-1865*	*B.C.*
Prabhas Patan	*TF-1286*	*1953*	*B.C.*
Rojdi	*PRL-1091*	*2867-2699*	*B.C.*
-do-	*TF-1087*	*2675-2515*	*B.C.*
-do-	*TF-199*	*1947*	*B.C.*
Somnath (Pd.I)	*TF-1287*	*2065-2860*	*B.C.*
-do-(Pd.II)	*PRL-92*	*2425-2155*	*B.C.*
Surkotada	*PRL-85*	*2940-2540*	*B.C.*
-do-	*TF-1305*	*2555-2285*	*B.C.*

After Possehl 2000

Some calibrated radiocarbon dates of the Late Harappan (1900 B.C.-1500B.C.)

Site	*Sample No.*	*Radiocarbon Dates*	*Calibrated Dates*
Daimabad (Pd. II)	*PRL-426*	*1760±155 bc*	*1961 cal. B.C.*
Daimabad (Pd. III)	*PRI-657*	*1285±105 bc*	*1424 cal. B.C.*
Daimabad	*BS-182*	*1275±95 bc.*	*1420 cal. B.C.*
Kalibangan	*TF-138*	*1215±105 bc*	*1391, 1334, 1327 cal. B.C.*
Kalibangan	*TF-152*	*1725±130 bc*	*1923 cal. B.C.*
Katelai (Late Bronze) bones	*R-476*	*1295±155 bc*	*1428 cal. B.C.*
Loebnar II (Pd. IV)	*P-2584*	*1285±60 bc*	*1424 cal. B.C.*
Mohenjo-daro (Late Mature)	*TF-75*	*1760±115 bc*	*1961 cal. B.C.*
Prabhas Patan	*PRL-19*	*1245±165 bc*	*1406 cal. ±B.C.*
Rojdi	*RF-191*	*1750±105 bc*	*1947 cal. B.C.*
Sibri (Period VIIIC)	*BETA-26*	*1365±60 bc*	*1514 cal. B.C.*
Shortughai (Pd. III)	*NY-424*	*1325±345 bc*	*1445 cal. B.C.*

All C^{14} dates after Sudha Satawadi 1994

Appendix 3

Table 1: Site Counts, Total Settled Area and Average Site Size for Sites of the Indus Age

Phase/Period	*Site counts measured*	*Settled area in ha*	*Average size in ha*
Post-urban Harappan c. 1900-1400 B.C.	*1281*	*4484*	*3.5*
Mature Harappan c. 2700-1900 B.C.	*1022*	*7358*	*7.2*
Early/Mature Harappan Transition c. 2700-2600 B.C.	*Insufficient settlement data*		
Early Harappan c. 3500-2800 B.C.	*477*	*2146*	*4.5*
Kechi Beg/Hakra Wares c. 3800-3200 B.C.	*256*	*1331*	*5.2*
Togau c. 4300-3800 B.C.	*84*	*294*	*3.5*
Burj Basket-marked c.5000-4300 B.C.	*33*	*86*	*2.6*
Kili Ghul Mohammad c. 7000-5000 B.C.	*20*	*52*	*2.6*

After Possehl 2000

Table 2: Site Counts, Total Settled Area and Average Site Size for Cholistan

Period	*Site counts*	*Settled area in ha*
Early Iron Age (Painted Grey Ware) c. 1600-500 B.C.	*14*	*36*
Post-urban Harappan (Cemetery H) c. 1900-1700(?) B.C.	*50*	*255*
Mature Harappan c.2700-1900 B.C.	*174*	*974*
Early Harappan (Kot Dijian) c.3500-2600 B.C.	*40*	*256*
Hakra Wares c.3800-3200 B.C.	*99*	*643*

After Possehl 2000 & Mughal 1997

Table 3: Chronology of Harappan

Phase/Period	*Site counts measured*	*Settled area in ha*	*Average*
Post-urban Harappan c. 1900-1400 B.C.	*1281*	*4484*	*3*
Mature Harappan c. 2700-2000 B.C.	*1022*	*7358*	*7*
Early/Mature Harappan Transition c. 2700-2600 B.C.	*Insufficient settlement data*		
Early Harappan c.3500-2800 B.C.	*477*	*2146*	*4*
Kechi Beg/Hakra Wares c. 3800-3200 B.C.	*256*	*1331*	*5*
Togau c. 4300-3800 B.C.	*84*	*294*	*3*
Burj Basket-marked c. 5000-4300 B.C.	*33*	*86*	*2*
Kili Ghul Mohammad c. 7000-5000 B.C.	*20*	*52*	*2*

After Possehl 20[illegible]

Bibliography

Agarwal D.P.	2000	Archaeo-materology and Archaeology of South Asia
Alchin FR. & Knox R	1981	Preliminary Report on the excavation at Tarakai Quila (1978-79) in H. Haertel (ed) S.A.A. 1979, Berlin.
Alchin FR	1984	The northern limits of the Harappan culture Zone in B.B. Lal and S.P. Gupta eds *Frontiers of the Indus Civilization,* Delhi.
Ardelenu Jansen Alexandra	1987	The Sherioanthromophic Stone Sculpture Mohenjo-daro in M. Jansen (ed) *Report on Mohenjodoro.* Interim Reports, Vol. 2, Rome
Ardelenu Jansen Alexandra	1984	Stone Sculpture from Mohenjo-daro in M. Jansen and G. Urban (ed) 1984: 139-47, Interim Reports, Vol. 1, Rome
Ardelenu Jansen Alexandra	1989	A Short note on a steatite sculpture from Mohenjo-daro *SAA 1985*: 196-210,London
Ardelenu Jansen Alexandra	1991	The Sculpture, art of the Harappa Culture in Jansen (ed) et,al 1991: 166-78, Berlin.

Ardelenu Jansen Alexandra	2002	The terracotta figurine from Mohen-Jodaro protohistory Archaeology of the Harappan Civilization ed. S. Settar, Delhi.
Ardelenu Jansen Alexandra	1992	New evidence of terracotta from Mohenjodaro in S.A.A. 1989, Madison
Atri Shubhangana	1986	Lady of Beasts - The Harappan Goddess in *Puratattva* No. 16,PP 7-13, Delhi.
Anthony D.	1995	The birth of the Chariot *Archaeology 48(2).* 36-41.
Bhattacharya, S.K.	1985	Indus Valley Art in *Masterpieces National Museum* ed S.P. Gupta, Delhi
Banerjee S	1973	Remain of the great one horned Rhinoceros from Rajasthan in *Science and Culture,* New Delhi.
Banerji Arundhati	1994	Proto Historic Indian Terracotta Art, New Delhi.
Banerji Arundhati	2000	Terracotta Art of North Western region Early Harappan and Mature Harappan period. Delhi
Bokonyi S.	1996	Horse remaims from Surkotada, Kutch late 3rd millennium B.C. in *South Asian Studies* 13:297-307
Bisht R.S	1991	Dholavira: A new horizon of the Indus Civilization *Puratattva 20*: 71-82, New Delhi.
Bhan K.K. & others	2002	Some important aspect of the Harppan technological tradition protohistory archaeology of the Harappan civilizaton eds. S. Settar.
Bisht R.S. & Joshi J.P.	1994	India & Indus Civilization, Delhi.
Bisht R.S.	1976	Banawali, (leaflet) Chandigarh, Department of *Archaeology,* Haryana.
Chang K.C.	1983	Art Myth and Ritual, Harvard,

Commarswamy A.K.	1927	Early Indian terracotta, *Bulletin of Museum of Fine Arts, Boston Vol. YXV.* Boston.
Dales G.E.	1985	Stone Sculpture from Proto historic Helmond Civilization, Afghanistan in *Tucci Memorial Vol.* Roma.
Dhavalikar M.K	1977	Master pieces of Indian Terracotta Art, Bombay,
Dikshit K.N	1979	Late Harappan Culture in India in *Essays in Indian Protohistory* ed B.M.pp Delhi.
Dikshit K.N	1983	Late Harappan culture in *Puratattva No.13 & 14* pp 51-61 New-Delhi.
Dikshit K.N.	1984	The Pre Harappan Culture of Rajasthan *Bharati Vol. II:55-70,* Varanasi.
During Caspers E.C.L.	1979	Caricature Grotesque and glamour in Indus Valley Art in S.A.A. 1977 ed M.Taddei.
During Caspers E.C.L.	1985(a)	The priest king from Mohenjodaro an Iconographic Assessment *AIVOM145:* 19-24 and P11-4.
During Caspers E.C.L.	1985(b)	More on the stone & sculpture from Mohenjodaro *AIVON 45*: 409-26 P11-6.
During Caspers E.C.L.	1985(c)	Sundry technical aspects of the Manufacture of Indus valley terracotta are in : *Gnoli and Laniotti Vol:*1267-85 P11-12
During Caspers E.C.L.	1986	Terracotta Artistry of Indus Valley in *A Ghosh M Volume II* ed B.M. Pande, PP 226-233 New Delhi.
During Caspers E.C.L.	1987	Linga Stones and gaming Board *AIVON47 (!)* : 67-74 and P111-8.
Dutta A.K.	1991	Unicornis : The great Indian one horned Rhino, Delhi.

Grigson C	1984	Some thoughts on Unicorns and other Cattle depicted at Mohenjo-daro and Harappa in S.A.A. Cambridge 1991.
Gupta S.P.	1996	Indus Saraswati Civilization, Delhi.
Jarrige Catherine	1983	The terracotta from Nindowari in S.A.A. 81
Jarrige Catherine	1991	Terracotta from Mehrgarh in *Forgotten Cities of Indus* ed Jansen
Jarrige Catherine	1992	Uneteted' elephant en terrecuitede Nausharo (Pakistan) in *Arts Asiatiques 47*: 132-36
Jarrige Catherine	1998	The Terracotta figurine from Nausharo in S.A.A. 1995, Parise.
Joshi J.P.	1982	Harappan culure emergence of New Picture, paper in *Puratattva, No. 13-14*, New Delhi.
Jayaswal Vidula & others	1998	Ethno-Archaeological view of Indian terracotta art, New Delhi.
Jayakar, Pupul	1980	The Earthen Drum, an introduction of Ritual art of India, New Delhi.
Kenoyer J.M.	1998	Ancient cities of Indus Valley Civilization, Islamabad
Lal B.B.	1997	The earliest civilization in South Asia, Delhi
Lal B.B.	2001	Saraswati flows on the continuity of Indian Culture, Delhi.
Mackey E.J.H.	1935	Chanhudaro excavations *A.R.A.S.I. 1935-36:38-34* Delhi
Mackey E.J.H.	1938	Further excavation at Mohenjodaro Vol. I-II, Delhi.
Marshall J.	1931	Mohenjodaro and Indus Civilization, Vol. I & II, Delhi.
Meadow R.H.	1997	A comment on Horse remain from Surkotada. late 3rd millenium B.C. in S.A.S. No. 13: 308-15.
Mughal M.R	1992(b)	The Geographical extent of the Indus civilization during the early, Mature, and late Harappan time in :Possehl 1992, 123-43.

Mughal M.R	1992(c)	The consequences of river changes for the Harappan settlement in Cholistan, in: *The Eastern Antra-Apologist 45* (1-2): 105-16
Nath J.	1991	Terracottas in the National Museum, Delhi.
Narain L.A. & Sharotri G.K	1980	Notes on the evolution techniques of Terracotta art in *National Museum Bulletin No.6*, P72, New Delhi.
Promod Chandra	1985	Sculpture of India from 3000 B.C. to 1300 A.D., Harvard
Pathak V.S.	1992	Buffalo-horned human figure on the Harappan Jar at Padri a note *M.E.17(1)*: 87-9.
Piggot. S.	1968	The earliest wheeled vehicles and the Caucasian evidence, P.P.S. 34: 2-318 London.
Postel Amy. G.	1986	From Indian Earth 4000 years of Terracotta art. The catalogue exhibition in Brooklyn Museum, U.S.A
Parpola A.	1994	Deciphering the Indus Script, New Delhi.
Possehl G.L	1999	The Indus Age the beginning, Delhi.
Ramamrutan Usha	1987	The Secret and the Secular art of Mohenjo-daro and Harappa, Vol. I. Bombay
Rao S.R.	1991	Dawn and Devolution of Indus Civilization, Delhi.
Rao S.R.	2001	The Lost City of Dvaraka, Delhi.
Sankalia H.D.	1978	Prehistoric art of India, New Delhi.
Sankalia H.D.	1990	Harappa Culture in Gujrat in ME 19 (1-7): 129-31
Shinde Vasant	1991(a)	A horn headed human figure on a Harappan Jar from padri Gujrat M.E. 16(2): 87-89.
Shinde Vasant	1991(b)	Harappan horned deity: the evidence from Padri in western India-*Puratattva* 21:79-81

Sarma I.K.& Singh B.P.	1967	The Terracotta Art of proto historic India in *Journal of Indian History Vol. 45*, pp 773-798.
San U.	1997	The Terracotta Art of Rajasthan pl. VI & VII, New Delhi.
Sharma A.K.	1974	*Evidence of Horse* from the Harappan settlement at Surkotada in *Puratattva no.* 7. pp.75-76 New Delhi.
Sharma A.K.	1993	The Harappan Horse was buried under the dunes in : *Puratattva No. 23*, pp.30-34, New Delhi.
Sharma D.P.	1999(a)	Harappan seals sealing and copper tablet, New Delhi.
Sharma D.P.	1999	(b) Indus script on the way to decipherment, Delhi
Sharma D.P.	1999 (c)	Some rare mother goddess terracotta figurines in the National Museum in *Prof. G. R.Sharma Vol* ed V.D.Misra Allahabad.
Sharma D.P. & Madhuri Sharna	2002	Mould made Indus Valley terracottas in National Museum Collection. In G.C. *Pande, Vol.* ed V.D. Misra Allahabad.
Sharma D.P	2002	Harappan Art Vol. I, Delhi.
Sharma D.P	2002(a)	Harappan Jewellery, Delhi.
Sharma D.P	2002(b)	Newly discovered copper hoard weapons of India, Delhi.
Shukla S.P.	1994	Harappan art heritage: A study paper in *W.A.C.3*, New Delhi.
Thapar B.K.	1989	Kalibangan I & II in E.I.A. Vol. II ed A.Ghosh, Delhi.
Tripathi V. & other	1994	Indus Valley terracotta art, New Delhi.
Vatsa M.S.	1940	Excavation at Harappa, New Delhi.
Sharma D.P.	Press	Harappan Archaeology till today - Delhi.
Sharma D.P.	2003	Archaeology of lower Ganga Yamuna doab. Delhi.

Sharma D.P. (ed)	Press	Harappan Civilization and some controversial Issues, Delhi.
Sharma D.P. (ed)	Press	Prehistoric Eastern South Asia and South East Asia a comparative study.
Sharma D.P. & Madhuri Sharma	2003	Roots of Ancient Indian Art of South Asia, Delhi.
Sharma D.P. (ed)	2003	Copper Hoard Weapon and O.C.P. Ceramics, Delhi.
Sharma D.P. & Others	Press	Minor Art and Craft of Harappan Vol I, II, III & IV.
Sharma D.P. & Kadambi	Press	Urban Planning and Settlement Pattern of Harappan. Delhi.
Sharma D.P. Sanjib Kumar Singh and Madhuri	2003	Prehistoric Archaeology of South Asia. Delhi.